CONSUMED
BY ONE ANOTHER

CONSUMED
BY ONE ANOTHER
The Black Race to Self-Destruction

DS
WALKER

CONSUMED BY ONE ANOTHER
THE BLACK RACE TO SELF-DESTRUCTION

iUniverse books may be ordered through booksellers or by contacting:

iUniverse
1663 Liberty Drive
Bloomington, IN 47403
www.iuniverse.com
1-800-Authors (1-800-288-4677)

Because of the dynamic nature of the Internet, any web addresses or links contained in this book may have changed since publication and may no longer be valid. The views expressed in this work are solely those of the author and do not necessarily reflect the views of the publisher, and the publisher hereby disclaims any responsibility for them.

Any people depicted in stock imagery provided by Thinkstock are models, and such images are being used for illustrative purposes only. Certain stock imagery © Thinkstock.

ISBN: 978-1-4917-5844-1 (sc)
ISBN: 978-1-4917-5846-5 (hc)
ISBN: 978-1-4917-5845-8 (e)

Library of Congress Control Number: 2015900774

Print information available on the last page.

iUniverse rev. date: 03/18/2015

It is not who we were
But who we are now.

It is about being honest with ourselves.
It is about falling in love with us again.
It is about abandoning our first love, God.

A letter from us to us.

I miss you, black.
I want cha back.

Contents

Preface

> But if you bite and devour one another, take care
> lest you be consumed by one another …
> —Galatians 5:15 NAS

I suppose I should find some well-known celebrity to write me a foreword in order to add credibility to my book. But then who would believe *me*? I'm just another black man running off at the mouth about something that every talk-show host or radio "celebrity" *call-in artist* has said for years. I'm not famous, just another voice in the crowd.

But then I thought to myself, *It really isn't about who's talking. It's really about who's listening.* It really doesn't matter who you are, if no one's listening, or, better yet, acts on what is being said. That makes us even. So, I might as well write my own.

We all now have the capacity and access to gain knowledge. Whose fault is it if you choose not to take advantage of it? Whose fault is it if you refuse to encourage others to as well? We have a responsibility not only to ourselves but also to those who are willing to listen. Most of our lives are spent being pushed and pulled in many "well-meaning" directions. The church's cry is that man's greatest problem is self-sufficiency. The very nature and purpose of humanity is to grow and to be able to stand on your own two feet, yet the concern in the church is that this could be destructive, and I can understand the point conveyed. However, for the sake of clarity, the very essence of life is that a bird, horse, child, or any other creature created by God learns to stand on its own and be self-sufficient. The problem doesn't seem to be self-sufficiency in and of itself. *That* is the goal for growth and maturity. The problem is that when we stand on our own in self-sufficiency, we refuse to allow our steps to be ordered by God, who *gave* us self-sufficiency, and we stand with our backs to the mirror.

Introduction

An introduction answers the question of why the author wrote the book and gives a glimpse into its contents. Well, here's why I wrote this book:

Life is so difficult regardless of the color of one's skin. Though I'm not *so* naive as to see that, for some, skin color does seem to allow advantages and the fantasy of superiority for one reason or another, but those delusions of superiority are, well, only skin deep. When that plane went into the buildings in New York, it didn't care about skin color. Terrorists don't shoot or blow up more black people than white people or any other "color" of people. Our biggest problems involve us as Americans more than what color we are, yet there is this infighting that distracts us from "enemies" that are nonprejudicial in their destruction of human life.

Now Rwanda disturbed me. These are Hutus and Tutsis who are the same color, yet there was genocide on a scale that boggles the mind. It was about superiority as well, differentiated by the size of one's nose and one's height. And what was to be gained in a country ravaged with poverty, unemployment, lack of education, and extreme health issues? But *this* is America. The melting pot of civilization. A land flowing with milk and honey. A land founded on religious convictions and whose founding fathers believed that God blessed this land and therefore its people, and God's principles were good enough to put a stamp on America. So where do we stand in this as black people? Have we not yet earned our existence on this quilt of America? Yes, we have. But now that we are here, regardless of how we got here, what are we doing with this privilege? I'm referring to this privilege of being an American, not the privilege of living in "white America." There is no white America, no more than there is a black Africa. It's just America.

This land, this world, belongs to no human
being, no color. It belongs to its Creator.
We are just renters behind on our rent to our land Lord.

So that brings us to *us*? What are we doing with this blessing? What must we do to get the most out of where we are? That is a question that only *we* can answer. Self-destruction is not the answer. Self-consumption out of frustration and fear is just fuel on the fire to a people who are so frustrated with our past and blaming white folks that we are destroying ourselves. We are our own Hutus and Tutsis.

Lastly, I want to make a comment on a very sensitive issue that has made headline news seemingly all over the world, especially in America. A subject that has brought on—or up again—the subject of race in America, that being the shooting and death of an unarmed seventeen-year-old black young man named Trayvon Martin at the hands of a thirty-year-old self-appointed neighborhood watch captain named George Zimmerman, who was later acquitted of all charges after a lengthy trial by an all (but one) white, female jury. Now, Mr. Zimmerman is identified as white and called in some articles—due to his father being white and his mother being Peruvian—a "white Hispanic." Also, there the unfortunate death of Michael Brown in Ferguson, Missouri, as well as all of the other "Martins" and "Browns" around the world. Without going through all of the specifics of these extremely sad and unfortunate losses of life, I want to focus on all of the interviews, comments, and statements that ooze out of wounds like these and express my disappointment on opportunities wasted but perhaps not yet missed.

While many are divided on racial lines about a situation that cannot be reversed at this point, I see this as a prime opportunity to discuss the issues we have *within* our own race. Of course all races could stand review, but let's focus on the black race. While people are making assessments of the need for legal justice in order to "make sure that this doesn't happen to another black child," the focus should be on fighting for two parents, relationships, and marriages and teaching our children more about life and how to handle conflict, racism, sexism, genderism, and all of the other isms that cause us to react in a confrontational manner. No, I am not blaming Trayvon Martin or Michael Brown for the actions of another or considering their plights as unimportant, but every action does cause a reaction. If we truly want this to not happen again, we need to teach our children to walk away, without seeing that as a sign of weakness. To make them understand that there are more important things in life than something that could potentially *take* your life or split up your family or cause division in a relationship, and for them to have a focus on something that they feel is so important that it is not worth a confrontation.

I will also say this, knowing that it will cause controversy: if you engage in unlawful activities or challenge authority, you must know that a possible consequential outcome of such deeds is punishment, injury or death, regardless of how it may come to happen. We must take ownership of our actions or of our contributions to actions taken place. Instead of black leaders salivating over revenge, they should be using this situation to refocus on looking deeply within ourselves, our race, our actions, and our legacy and making ourselves better able to deal with our past as black people, embracing and valuing love and family and each other.

We now have the attention of the next generation. *It is not for self-appointed leaders to overlook our own responsibilities for the sake of pointing out the injustices of others.* Our youth are watching the reactions of the adults that are ahead of them and how they handle bad and sometimes unfair situations like this. There will always be situations that will come up in our lives that we had no hand in creating or that are out of our control, but the resolution to *any* problem will always be in what we *can* control, which is our *reaction* to that problem. What an opportunity missed. Conflict, whether in dangerous situations, marriage, friendship, or working relationship, involves knowing yourself, your propensities, your hot buttons, and your limits. Conflict always involves someone else, though sometimes there are conflicts *within* that are far greater than the conflicts outside of us.

I just want to draw attention to *us*. That's why I wrote this book.

Imagine That.

The Three Thirty-Second, Ninety-Ninth,
Four Seventy-Seventh, Triple-Nickel, and Buffalo Soldiers.
Imagine that.
Lena Horn, Charles Drew, and James Baldwin.
Imagine that.
Born with ten fingers and ten toes and as cute as a button.
Imagine that.
My old couch, now on the corner under a tree, reeking with the smell of vomit, lies and dirty pampers stuffed between the filthy, bloodstained pillows.
Imagine that.
Thirteen and a gunshot, fourteen and a thump.
The sirens are deafening. Finally, the quiet of the single clang of a steel door. A funeral at nine.
Imagine that.
I smell hair burning. Someone's playing with the lights again.
Imagine that.
Wake up! Wake up! You're dreaming again! But it seemed so real. So real!
Imagine that.

—DSWalker

"Turn Around!"

Making the Elephant Disappear

How many times has it been suggested or have you as an African American been told to "pull yourself up by your own bootstraps"? What does this mean, really? Who is saying this and why? I'm not, at this point, questioning the validity of this statement, but to whom exactly is this statement directed? The statement is defined as the ability to achieve success by one's own *unaided* efforts—advice obviously given by one who has made this unaided achievement. I can see no other qualification for making such a statement. Does this piece of "advice" in all its splendor and magnificent wisdom come with an assumption that there are bootstraps to pull up? Or perhaps this is one of those game show deals that come with their own bootstraps. And do these bootstraps come with boots? Or are we once again asking for too much? Maybe I'm being too typical? Too cynical? Too critical? *Too black*?

Now, realizing that this is a generic statement, I can only address this statement from a black perspective. And while I am only exercising my right to my own opinion, this statement—in its real sense—crosses all cultural and ethnic bounds. However, as it crosses those bounds, very often the rules change.

Now, at the risk of being accused of stereotyping, I shall attempt to address this issue as I see it and from personal accounts, many of which are not exclusive to me. There are many issues in the American

Negro community that need to be, and can only be, addressed by American Negroes. I have spoken to groups, workers and anyone else who would give me an interested ear on the perspective of American Negro people. I in no way claim to be the voice of the people. I only speak for myself. I am also in no way offering any excuses for the downtrodden and oppressed of our society. For as many people, there are as many reasons. *Life is too precious to be measured by the length of a bootstrap.* To assume apathy is to deny empathy and declare separatism. It is no secret that the American Negroes' greatest enemy is an uneducated and undeveloped mind. Whether it is our own minds not realizing who we are and learning to respect that *and each other,* starting with yourself, or others who realize who we are better than we know ourselves but refuse to give us respect when it is earned and due, it makes no difference. The same mental tactics are playing American Negroes against each other now as were used to control our slave ancestors. And we are buying into it like a bag of bad weave. *Unbeweaveable!*

We do not need fresh and new ideas; we just need to use what we already have. But these ideas cannot be used if you're in a jail cell. These ideas cannot be used if your minds are clouded with drugs. These ideas cannot be used if parents choose to reward themselves to the point of indebtedness—wearing, living in, and driving their son or daughter's college education money and using the excuse that the cost of education is too high and that there is not enough money left to give their child a future. A future cannot be built on blaming White folks for our every fault and inability to *"make it in the white man's world."* Folks, we have a problem in *black America* that black America refuses to admit or recognize. There is an elephant so big in the room that we choose to go around it like the children of Israel in the wilderness as opposed to a straight line to milk and honey.

America was built on and is still supported by small businesses that later grow to be large corporations with influential people running them, otherwise known as capitalism. Black America refuses to accept the fact that we cripple ourselves with bad etiquette, poor customer service, shabby management skills, basic education, and a mind-set that seems to say that since we are now free from slavery and noncitizenship, there are certain jobs that we will not take because we are now bigger than that. We refuse to support our black businesses because we simply want to be treated like human beings by one another—"the way we see whites treating one another in the stores"—and our prices are too high even though we feel more comfortable spending more in white (and Asian) establishments because the water in the "whites only" fountain seems to taste better than the water in the "blacks only" fountain. When will we get past that? Wake up, black America. We have a problem! And it's not *all* "their" fault. Stop singing "We Shall Overcome" and overcome! We hurt ourselves much more than and have killed more of us than slavery did. Stop standing with your backs to the mirror! Turn around, and the elephant will disappear!

Does White America Get It?

Unresolved Issues

Though black America must solve its problems from the inside out, I am in no way making an attempt to let white America off the hook in being a contributor to the ineffectiveness of black America's ability to grow, achieve, and prosper in this great country we all wave our flags, sing songs, and go to war for. White America will continue to wave the flag of innocence to the slavery and atrocities our black forefathers have gone through, saying that this present and future generation of whites should not be blamed for the past. While that is true, it is not rocket science to see that this current and future generation of white Americans have and will continue to benefit from what their forefathers did to black people, and many of their successes were made directly from the backs of black slaves and inventions, which created this "old money" and influence that *current* and *future* generations of white Americans have and will continue to enjoy the fruits of without apology. This country and others have made an attempt to right the wrongs of every other atrocity but that of black America (e.g., China's refugee camps, Russia's war, Jewish people's Holocaust … all of which are very deserving due to their devastation but none of which lasted over four hundred years to a people who still have not recovered from and have not been "paid" for the physical and mental torture and brainwashing they endured).

As it is embedded into the minds of many white Americans that they are superior by design, it is unfortunately also embedded into the minds of many black Americans that they are inferior by design. While God does encourage forgiveness, ask first for repentance. There is a crime being ignored in America that prevents healing. An issue ignored.

This book was not written to cause division or anger but to continue the dialogue that is needed to promote healing and to move forward with needed progress. We live in very troubled times, and the greatest fear seems to be talking about our pain without being called racist, insensitive, or just plain, old wrong. *In our conversations on race, we will have to allow some tolerance of ignorance without anger and blame to give people the freedom to express their deepest feelings and concerns.* We need open minds and open hearts, and before a problem can be solved, there must first be an admission that there *is* a problem instead of hiding behind the wall of neutrality or masking our differences for fear of being looked at as different. Reverend Martin Luther King Jr. put it this way:

> Many people fear nothing more terribly than to take a position which stands out sharply and clearly from the prevailing opinion. The tendency of most is to adopt a view that is so ambiguous that it will include everything and so popular that it will include everybody. Not a few men who cherish lofty and noble ideals hide them under a bushel for fear of being called different.

Or for fear of being called out.

So, let's start the controversy.

Expression One

NO BOOTS

Identity:
Tangible versus Intangible Slavery

This Is About Us

African American? I don't think so! The first step at making progress seems to be in first knowing *what* we are before we start figuring out *who* we are. Contrary to the suggestions of Jesse Jackson and others—all due respect to them all—we are not African Americans. Most true African people that I talk to see a very distinct difference between black people born in America and people born in Africa, as well as first-generation Africans here in America. That true African ancestral blood has thinned out from Africa to America so much that—outside of our color and distinctive physical attributes—we are a race of people different from any other race on this planet. The only thing we have in common is living in America, and compared to most of the world, America is a great place to live. However, having ancestry in Africa does not an African make black people in America.

There was, as I wrote this, a very real controversial situation going on that supports my debate. It's called the census. There was a call in to a local radio station to some representatives of a census support group, and the question, of which I was happy to hear, involved what ethnic box to check to identify their race. They were white people born and raised in Africa but now residing in America. The selections on the census were white, black, African

American, or Negro. You take a stab at it! They were white, but that's a race, and that does not identify an origin. They are Africans, but they are not black or Negro. They are African Americans. African Americans are people—black, white, or whatever—born in Africa but residing in America as their new home as citizens. That label does not distinguish black people. I am more in line with James Baldwin who refers to us as American Negroes. We are in effect more of a hybrid than pure African. Does that make us inferior? No! It makes us special.

Most of who we are comes from the African lineage in us. How far back do you suggest we run our lineage in order to be considered African? Let's face it; most of us stretched that African blood out to zero many generations ago. Can you really *go back* to Africa? Perhaps it's a conspired psychological disfranchisement to make black people feel like a bastard race. In the book *From Slavery to Freedom: A History of Negro Americans,* by John Hope Franklin, there's a line that says, "Once the Negro was disfranchised, everything else necessary for white supremacy could be done." America is home, folks! Don't be denied. We've spent years, tears, and lives fighting for our rights as black citizens here in America as well as in wars for this country, yet we call Africa our homeland. While it is indeed our roots, and I love that, and I love Africa and hold a spot near and dear in my heart for the place where civilization began, I live in America. I have been to Africa. I'll speak on that later. However, we have one foot in the boat and one foot in the water. I demand my rights right here in America, not Africa. I carry its name. Black people are Negroes born in America. American Negroes. Don't be disfranchised. If the boot fits, wear it.

It never ceases to amaze and astound me that Negroes in America have only been free (the ability to enjoy the fruits of your labor and property, to vote, ride the bus, look up while you walk in public, eat where you want to, all without risk of open and overt retaliation) for almost less time than my age. Now, read that opening statement again and take just a moment to think about that. Go ahead. I'll give you a moment …

The Civil Rights Act was just signed in 1964! Prior to 1964, we as American Negroes were here for someone else's purpose and use in most of this country. But slavery and being indentured was not created two hundred to four hundred years ago. There has been slavery since the days of the Bible. It was allowed by God Himself. God wasn't so much concerned about the capturing of the body as much as He was the capturing of the mind. They were there because they were taught and believed that that was where they belonged, and so they accepted that. You can't just tell an elephant to stop. An elephant will stop only because it decides in its own mind to stop, when and only when it feels there is a reason that warrants it to stop, unless you kill it, trap it, or chemically subdue it. And with that, you only stop the body, not the mind, which means you have changed nothing permanently.

Slavery in and of itself is not the issue. While God allowed it to exist, He also gave specific instructions as to how this slave or indentured servant was to be treated. And that is where slavery gave American Negroes that dreaded "wedgy" that has *still* got us wiggling when we walk. You see, slavery was a physical act. A tangible confinement. You could see it and touch it. How you were treated was a mental act. Which stays with you longer? It was something that dug into your mind deeper than that whip dug into your skin. An intangible confinement. You couldn't touch it, yet the feel of it stayed with you longer than even the sting of that whip. *Had black people been stolen as servants against their will and treated wonderfully and respectfully but without physical freedom, it would have been called an opportunity instead of slavery.*

My momma always told me something that many a mom has whispered to many a child: "It's all about how you treat a person, son. It's about how you talk to a person 'cause God don't like ugly."

We've made great strides as American Negroes. That cannot be denied. However, the Atlantic Ocean will always look upon Erie as just another lake. That is unless and until Lake Erie can find a way to connect to it and become a part of it. The Bible has a saying, "The devil can't stand against itself." Not and survive too. Connecting creates a need for one another. Then when you hurt, he'll hurt. It is only then the pain stops. No one wants to hurt him or herself. Every boot needs a foot, and every foot needs a boot. It's called economics. I like survival better. I like *Love* even better.

The Unnatural Need to Be Needed

Love is going take some time and work. You see, love is the purest expression of the "need to be needed." When love is missing, you can kill each other with guns and destroy each other with drugs (it use to be called dope, but I guess that sounded too offensive to people and offended users). I'm not as concerned about what white people did to us during slavery because I'm more concerned about what we are doing to ourselves while we are free. What we as American Negroes do to each other is not only unexplainable but unnatural and done through a lack of knowledge of who we are. It's like a pit bull trained to be violent, and each offspring somehow inherits part of that teaching, mixing it up with survival or expected behavior. But what we do, we do to each other more than not. Why do we turn on each other? *That* is unnatural. I realize that it is unnatural for *any* human being to turn on any other human being, but when it's put in the context of an entire race of people, it becomes more suspect. Could it be that we have been so brainwashed into thinking that we are worthless that when we harm each other, we subconsciously see it as getting back at *us* for being *us*? No big deal. No value. No harm done. Just trash throwing out trash? Do we hate ourselves for being hated? When told to pull ourselves up by our own bootstraps, do we look down and see that we have no boots, then get angry and strike out at the only ones we can reach, *us*? How can you pull yourself up by that which you don't have? And who is to blame for no boots?

Have we not been free enough long enough to have gotten us some boots? So why does this statement bother American Negroes so?

Boots represent possession, power, and ownership. They represent a measure of independence and a measure of a step, if you will, in not just the right direction but in *any* direction. They identify you as being a part of the whole. No boots, no part. No justice, No peace. They represent knowledge and independence and acceptance. So go and pull yourself up by your own knowledge and independence, and "we" will accept you.

I was questioned in great frustration one day by a black associate as to why it is that white America has such a hold on corporate ownership, politics, and seemingly somehow control on every front? It was suggested to me by this person that it seemed that no matter how high an American Negro goes in this country, there's a white person higher up the ladder, controlling the major decisions. Now while I fail to see the surprise or shock in that, I could very well understand the frustration it causes. And I did not take that statement as an indictment against white America. It was a fair assessment. White roots run deep. I have a number of white associates, and I cherish their friendship. We learn from one another—unfortunately, many times in a very guarded way so as to not "offend" one another. This is done to keep from damaging what is still looked upon as a fragile kinship. We marry into one another's family but not into one another's lives or backgrounds. Keep in mind the opening paragraph of this expression. We had no roots prior to 1964, at least none that were openly expressed or socially accepted. We've always had something cooking underneath. We redefined the words *underground* and *black market*.

White America has had control ever since they infiltrated America. Those trees started from the surface down, and those roots run deep. Would we have been any different had the tables been turned? What would Shaka Zulu say about that? And exactly what is being controlled? Remember my earlier piece on physical and mental slavery? Cause and effect. But the solution is simple.

If our counterpart friends have roots too deep to get at, grow your own trees. Get you some roots, your own roots. Stop complaining about what white folk got or won't give you! If you can't fix it, get for yourself a new one!

God's word in Psalm 103:9 (NAS) says that His spirit would not strive with us always. That we truly do not get all that we deserve for the wrongs we do in life. The book of Genesis 6 tells us that God was well aware of the fact that His spirit inside all of us was being corroded away by the ways of the world and would eventually be quenched by our own selfish desires over His. This struggle between spirit and flesh would wage such a war for so long that man would eventually fall to a level of which God would not contend with. The Holocaust in the 1930s and 1940s was all about genocide. An intentional effort to murder a people thought to be useless in their particular environment, along with the fear of their children growing up to be a threat to those who destroyed their past. The Lodz Ghetto and the Warsaw Ghetto were the beginnings of true ghettos. There seemed to be no limits to man. Of course, before that was black slavery and the intentional attempt of the genocide of the American Indian. The interesting theme of these times, after reading about and watching documentaries on these events, was that we had been convinced that the people mentioned above were not human, which gave them the ease of mind to commit these atrocities. In Rwanda, the enemies were known as cockroaches. Where was religion and where was democracy during these times? Where are they now? That's what a broken soul does to people. Our only hope is to know who our enemy truly is and defeat it with love. Starting with us. Lest we be consumed.

Get You Some Roots!

American Negroes are just beginning to grow roots, but once those roots are down, we must keep them. Cultivate them. Nurture them. Learn from them. Pass them on to our children instead of selling off—or out—to old roots. But are our children ready to be handed this responsibility? You should know; you raised them! *Now* who are you going to blame? Hello! Hello! These are things that must be learned from either education or experience, both of which we have access to and plenty of. But you know what they say about power in the hands of a fool—fool meaning uneducated or inexperienced.

First order of business is to get the boots. Left boot is called Education. Right boot is called Economics. However, before we go too far, let's understand the very real possibility that we can be rubbed raw with education and experience. How many people do you know with plenty of education and experience that cannot mentally deal with the pressures of obstacles set before them? You've got adequate supply of both but still seem to get no respect. Well, while there are indeed outside circumstances and cases for this, let's look in the mirror first. Who do you see? Ask yourself, "Who am I? Why am I?" Let's call these questions socks.

Surely no one puts on boots without socks. That's assuming you have boots of course. That assumption is founded on the fact that there must be boots or these intellectuals would not be asking you to pull yourself up by the straps. The left sock is called Identity, and the right sock is called Purpose. The left sock, identity, fits into the left boot we call education. An inseparable combination. They need each other to be whole and complete and the best they can be. *To be educated and not know who you are is as dangerous as knowing who you are and not being educated.* There's a fool in there somewhere.

Education comes in many forms, however. There's institutionalized education, such as schools, churches, gangs, and prisons. There's noninstitutionalized education, such as the streets or being streetwise, having wit and being conniving, and learned survival techniques. It all boils down to choices. While the tendency is to say that unfortunately most of the wrong choices are made, I think that's not the case. It's just that the wrong ones usually get the spotlight or front page. That doesn't make it the norm. We've got to understand that. We've got to understand who we are as a people. To learn about our own very significant contributions and freely accept the contributions of others. All others. Most of the hurt and pain inflicted by American Negroes is inflicted on other American Negroes. And while that doesn't make it right, we would be hard pressed to name an American Negro who has assassinated an American president, or who was a serial killer, or who sent mail bombs or set off bombs that killed hundreds of innocent lives, or who through their greed for wealth or political power singlehandedly affected millions of lives by influencing the GNP, stock markets, inflation, big-business decisions and directions, property taxes, and legislation, or one with the power and significance to import the abundance and proliferation of drugs into this country, which mysteriously ends up in the neighborhoods, hands, noses, and arms of young and otherwise potentially gifted and society-contributing American Negroes. It creates pain that ripples through generations. It takes power and influence to do those kinds of things. And not necessarily real power. There's that power I call *assumption by affiliation.* Makes my back hurt just thinking about it. This is not a personal or racial indictment. It's only an opinionated dialogue meant to illuminate the fact that when one finger points at someone, the other fingers – more fingers - point back at you. Repent and sin no more.

The right foot has the sock of purpose and the boot of economics. If you put the two together, it forms a question. "What do you do with your money?" During our ancestors' physical slavery, they fought to be physically free. During our political slavery, we fought to be politically free (put it in writing). We now have two more hurdles to overcome. Neither are things to be given to us. Both are things we simply need to realize. The first is our mental freedom, and the second is our economic freedom. The reality of these seems to be threatening, but reality need not be threatening, only recognized. The buzzword nowadays is *power,* and power only recognizes control.

A thought: There is but one ultimate, effective, and recognizable definition of power, and that is the power to control (the minds and/or thoughts of) people. It's not about money or fame or unusual intellect or profession; it's about the power to control people. Choose your weapon(s) carefully.

To attempt to pick yourself up by that which you don't have is no different from attempting to pick yourself up by that which you do have but is not recognized or accepted as yours or, at the very least, yours as a contributor. Allow me to end this expression with a representative interpretive expression not fully my own. It is said and seemingly backed by educated ignoramuses that the intelligence of whites is higher than that of blacks (as is assumed Asians are of whites). This seems to have the agenda if not to perpetuate the myth, to certainly further separate the disrespect and ill feelings between American Negroes and European Americans (American whites). Although the basis of such will always be disputed, the notion can be played with that white Americans *should be* "smarter" considering the fact that they have learned about their culture and history since day one in American. The opposite is true for the American Negro and his history. And if there is a problem with accepting the well-established contributions of the American Negro by white America, and if indeed the bell curves toward the advantaged whites in America, then perhaps they should not answer their phones when they ring in their homes and businesses and public places because a black man (Lewis Howard Latimer, employed by Alexander Graham Bell to create the patent drawings for the first telephone) had something strategic to do with that. Don't bother telling your loved ones to even turn on that auto turn signal (invented by R. B. Spikes, a black man) just so that you can ignore that traffic light (invented by Garret A. Morgan, a black man), the perils of which could cause a nasty accident that could land you in the hospital with the need for that life-saving stored blood (plasma) transfusion (efficiently stored by the pioneering efforts of Dr. Charles Drew, a black man), which would have kept you from getting to work in that office building pleasurably equipped with an elevator trusted and controlled (by a device produced by J. Cooper, a black man) to get you to your floor and at your work station on time, recognized by the clock on the wall (there because of the inventor of the first clock in America, Benjamin Banneker, who, by the way, in his spare time was the blueprint planner for Washington, DC, America's capital). It is the same kind of clock that sets off the lunch bell at your child's school, which allows him or her to enjoy that peanut butter and jelly sandwich (thanks to George Washington Carver and his three hundred other products from the peanut and the sweet potato) taken out of that paper bag (produced because of the inventor of the paper bag machine, William B. Purvis, a black man) while you enjoy a nicely cooked piece of meat (probably brought to your grocer by refrigerated railroad cars and trucks, invented by Frederick McKinley Jones, a black man). This lunch will have to tide you over until after work so that you can then enjoy yourself by either mowing the lawn (inventor of the lawn mower, J. A. Burr, a black man), releasing a little energy by going to the rodeo to watch a little bulldogging (invented by a black cowboy Hall-of-Famer, Bill Pickett) or just relax with a couple rounds of golf (inventor of the golf tee, George F. Grant, a black man) or just go to bed. Don't forget to turn off the lights (inventor and patentee of the first incandescent electric lightbulb with a carbon filament was the chief draftsman for both the General Electric and Westinghouse Companies, Lewis Howard Latimer, a black man). Déjà vu? Sweet dreams. The lights are off, and everything is Negro. Sorry, I meant black. Goodnight. In the end, does it really matter? But for the grace of God.

Expression Two

BOOTS AND NO STRAPS

Freedom and the Weaker Brother's Conscience

Having boots and no straps is like having parents who don't hug you. You feel like you really have something special, but you can't extract its full potential. It's like having a computer without knowing much about computers. It gets so frustrating to have something of such value without the ability to fully utilize it. So you began to take the boots for granted. You walk in them, trip and fall, and blame yourself for not being able to adapt. You get upset with yourself because you can't quite make the unusual usual. You can't make the abnormal normal. And what is even worse is that you think you should. Perhaps this is all you know. No one ever says, "Pick yourself up by your own boots." It's always the boot*straps* that you must clasp in your clinched fists and pull to a point of satisfaction. But to whose satisfaction?

There is a story in the Bible, more specifically the book of First Corinthians, chapter 10, for those brave enough to venture, about an invitation to dinner by one who is "different." The main concern, in one interpretation, was the acceptance and adaptation into the life of the other. How to behave on another's turf, or in another's world, not realizing that this world is just another room in the same house. What can I say and how do I say it without seeming insensitive or unappreciative? And, Lord, what about the food? You see, while one was overly concerned, they both needed to free each other. You'll really need to read that chapter for some background, but through this ordeal, a very interesting and provocative question was asked, seemingly out of frustration. That question was: "Why is my freedom judged by another's conscience?" Ponder that for a minute or two before going on. I'll give you some time …

Can you be poor *and* happy? To some, that is abnormal or unusual. I assume that to be the thinking of the rich and unhappy. There's a lot of that going around these days, you know. What a pity. We could very easily trade them some poor for some happiness. It's called love, and it goes both ways. So who is this *we* I so stereotypically suggested could trade some poor for some happiness? There I go putting a color on trouble again. My bad!

The Sunday, May 21, 1995, edition of the *Dallas Morning News* had an article in its books section written by Norman Oder, entitled "Bootstraps Have No Race" and subtitled "Professor says self-reliance is the best tool for blacks." *For blacks* is the focal point here. Now Mr. Oder was mainly focusing on some quotes by a Mr. Loury, professor of economics at Boston University, who opposed many leaders of the civil rights establishment on the ground of them "discounting the role of "values, social norms and personal attitudes" but instead focuses on black-on-black crime and disregarding the importance of school. He also added that black leaders "won't condemn men who father children but don't support them." Another child going un-hugged? Surely they can't be self-reliant. They'll need to be taught values, social norms, and personal attitude adjustments. All without straps. The value of boots without straps. The social norms and graces of learning and conforming to a new way of walking in those strapless boots. And arguably the most important factor is the ability to adjust your personal attitude to deal with the ridicule and lack of understanding by others to be encountered. But that's nothing new to the American Negro. The question is: have we adjusted to the state of worthiness or worthlessness? If I may put it that way, and I will. But for the grace of God.

There was a very disturbing statement made by William Bennett, former secretary of education under the Reagan administration and director of drug control policy under George H. W. Bush (research the Internet for validation or go to the MediaMatters.org interview). It was another attempt to reinforce the worthlessness and "re-chaining" the minds of black people. In an interview, he was asked for ways to deter crime in America. His answer was to "abort every black baby in this country and this crime rate would go down …" inspired by the book *Freakonomics* (William Morrow, May 2005). Make no mistake about it, the year was 2005, and the median was television and radio. The man was white. Remember, I said two more hurdles to overcome. Mental freedom and economic freedom. We are not the only ones who realize this need. When one is attacked, it usually means we are getting closer to what's important to someone else. Too close. Don't miss that!

Earning Your Straps

Boots with no straps is also like having authority with no power. Sound familiar? Thinking about your job maybe? You're looking good every day, or at least appropriate for your occupation, and you know your job and do it well, or at the very least just as good as (you fill in the blank). You may even have a title: administrator, VP of finance, group manager, shift manager, personnel and human resource manager. There is this misleading assumption or saying in the black community going around nowadays in the hoods of America. And please note that the "hoods of America" does not only refer to the slums of your favorite city. The hoods of America refers to any place where there is a number of disrespected, hardworking, second-class citizens assembled for survival in a place of either their own choosing with no respect or a place not chosen but without immediate recourse. That could be a downtown high-rise, a specific sector of town, or the maids' quarters in an exclusive suburban mansion. The saying handed down that I am referring to is "American Negroes must be twice as good as whites in all that is done—not only to get ahead but to be as good as." Now, as I heard this saying drummed into the fibers of my psyche, I began to form a picture in my mind of myself in a field, tired, sweaty, hungry, thirsty, and mentally exhausted, with a shovel in my hand, digging a whole deep enough for an average-size man to stand upright in. This was my hood. This was my job. But as I panned my view, to the left side of me I noticed a hole dug and completed already. As I viewed the right of me, I saw a white person next to me working just as hard, just as tired, just as sweaty, just as hungry, just as thirsty and mentally exhausted as I was. At the front of each hole was a sign with the name of the person on it who dug it. However, I couldn't see the names from where I was standing. The whistle blew, signifying the end of the workday, and everyone lined up in front of a booth to receive the day's pay. The white person walked up, got his hundred-dollar pay, a firm handshake, a smile, and pat on the back for a job well done by the boss. I stepped up, got my hundred dollars, a firm handshake, a smile, and a pat on the back for a job well done also.

So I walk away thinking to myself, *A good day's pay for a good day's work and time to go and feed my family.* But as I started to walk out, I couldn't help but glance back at my triumphant labor, otherwise known as "the hole," and to my dismay and confusion, the completed hole to the left of me had my name on it, as did the hole just to the right of it. The white person's name was only on the one hole to the right of my second hole. I glanced down at the hundred-dollar bill in my hand, sliding it through my finger and thumb, trying to separate what was to me obviously two bills stuck together. Alas, there was only one. I went back to the boss and explained the mistake and asked for my hundred dollars for the second hole I had dug, to which he replied very calmly and very matter-of-factly that it was a very well-known fact that American Negroes must work twice as hard as whites for the same benefits. I told him that I never agreed to that, to which he responded, "Neither did I, but that's just the way it is. That's what black people have come to believe and value as their measure of success, and we accept that on your behalf." And in the words of Homie the Clown, "I don't think so!" We should all work twice as hard.

However, I cannot even begin to sight the faults of societal wrongs before I point out wrongs of our own.

Earning your straps is a far-reaching endeavor that is not *given* to anyone and in many ways is not even something you earn but is mostly something you learn. Let's start with the basic foundation of democratic economics. A capitalistic society unfortunately. It's called the relationship between customers and your paycheck."

One day I went to get some gasoline from a service station I frequented a lot. While I was there, I decided to get some long overdue work done on my pickup. A small job, but the consequences of not getting it done would far outweigh the cost. I had been driving my truck without a spare for some time because either someone clipped the bottom cable and took it (it's held underneath the back cab, as it is most trucks) or it broke off and my spare fell off while driving. Repairing it meant reinstalling a brace that cranks the spare tire down. My problem was that I could not get the two bolts off with the tools I had, so while I was at the service station, I decided I'd get the mechanic to do the job for me. It would be cheaper than calling a wrecker on a lonely, dark street with my kid and a flat tire, and he makes a small profit. I believe the auto repair portion of this service station was rented and independently run by two American Negro men. I approached one of them, who was cordial and said he'd do it, but his approach said, "When I feel like it," but at least he addressed it. There were a couple other cars ahead of me, so I took out a book and waited. The other black American mechanic later came out. He spoke with a more vested interest (in the shop, not in me). He saw me waiting and with a grimace asked me what I was waiting for. So I showed him my new part and explained to him what I needed done. He picked up the part with a frown, looked at me, handed me back the part, and said to me (and I quote), "I ain't got time for this. I can't make no money on this," and simply walked off to another customer with an assumed bigger and more profitable problem. Now, the other guy was at least forcefully cordial even though his intentions were not exactly expeditious. But the other brother's response put such a bad taste in my mouth that I left the station with no real intent to even go back there for gas.

Now let me sum up the real problem with this whole scenario because this seems to be a very typical response in many establishments either owned or worked by American Negroes. I have a very sensitive side when it comes to customer service. I value good customer service, and I'll tell you why, which I believe is one of the biggest reasons African American businesses are not supported by American Negroes. "We want to be treated like human beings!" Doesn't that statement sound frighteningly familiar? Not only does this put a bad taste in the mouths of our own people but even more importantly it affects the very survival of a host of people relying on the paychecks of that business. You can go into seemingly any establishment where the workers are American Negroes, and unfortunately more times than not you'll receive poor customer service. Does this mean whites only give good customer service? No! Is this an indictment on all black businesses? No! I am now only focusing on a very sensitive and controversial issue that seems to be taboo, especially when it looks like a brother is ragging on brothers. It's got nothing to do with one dissin' another. It's economics!

The adult proprietor at that service station has the same problem that is pervasive in the minds of our youth. It's called the Taking the Cart Before the Horse syndrome. We as a society have grown to be one who wants seemingly something for nothing. More for less. We want the goodies before we are willing to work and plan for them. The thought at the gas station should have been to help me and satisfy me as best he could, not for the small amount of profit versus time invested now but for what is known as residual profits. That's the money he'll make from me when I come back for bigger jobs for him to do for me because he treated me so well on the last job. Good customer service today means more profits tomorrow, not only from me but from those that I recommend to him because he did such a good job for me. There is no excuse for bad customer service no matter what color you are or your personal problems. If we as American Negroes expect to work with one another, we must treat one another better than those who treat us badly. Hello! The ultimate reason behind it is our failure to respect the simple connection between customers and profits. An extension of the dreaded CP (colored people) time.

$$C_{ustomers} = P_{rofits} = Paycheck = Eat$$

No customers = No cha-ching! =
No company = No paycheck = No eat

It's a straight line. It's not rocket science!

Treating customers badly can have a detrimental effect on your eating schedule. It's the ultimate diet. You will indeed slim down faster. Even if it's not your company, you cannot just go into work to pass the time away, waiting on payday. Know it or not, you, Mr. and Mrs./Ms. employee, have an effect on generating that check you *didn't* earn each payday. That business's reputation revolves around the impression customers get from you, the employee. The employees get their impressions from the leader. I would much rather work for a leader than a boss any day. A boss tells you what to do. A leader shows you what to do. We need more leaders and fewer bosses. Think about it!

There is a huge problem in black America, an elephant so big in the room we choose to go around it and pretend it's not there rather than deal with it. While this statement does not go to all of black America, it certainly stains all of us. We are by percentage very unprofessional in work etiquette, practice, and customer service. Most are very good at their craft, but that is where it ends. The reason that this stains all of black America is because we as American Negroes allow our people to be that way. We must demand better! But for the grace of God.

Expression Three

BOOTS AND STRAPS

Don't Walk

One sunny spring day I went downtown to look for a comfortable place to settle, study, and think in order to prepare myself for a promotional interview I was scheduled for later that evening. I had gone on a couple of interviews before for either the same type or similar positions and didn't make the cut. I didn't personally feel that I had done anything wrong that caused me not to get the position, so I was going to prepare for this one the same as I had the prior ones. Yes, I felt a little slighted for racial reasons, but I, along with a lot of other American Negroes, get tired of bumping into this same reason for not making the cut even though I and many others know that discrimination and bias were most definitely a big part of the reason. Many people, white and black ironically, felt that this was also the reason for my not getting selected and suggested I pursue some sort of EEO or discrimination suit, but I simply didn't want that because I knew that I was good enough and could without a doubt do the job. This made me even more determined to keep knocking at the door until they had no choice but to know that I was the best choice. So I went downtown to brush up.

Walking downtown in any major city in the world is a similar experience. There are the homeless, the hustle and bustle, and short tempers. I came to a crosswalk that had the Walk light flashing in my direction, but about halfway across, the Don't Walk light came on, as it often does with many people. There was a green minivan poised to make a left turn but waiting for me to get clear. As I got

33

clear enough for the van to make its turn (and I was rushing), the driver rolled down his window slightly and shouted at me, "Nigger, can't you read? The sign says don't walk, nigger!" (Note: nigger should never be given the respect of being capitalized, unless at the beginning of a sentence of course. It, in my opinion, does not qualify as a proper noun.) He then did as people like that usually do, rolled his window up and drove on.

When I got to a quiet place, my mind was clouded because of this incident. I lost my concentration, and my self-esteem was questioned. Racism doesn't anger me as much as it confuses me. I had gone through that day being a model citizen to people of all races and religions—literally giving up my bus seat to a white woman, holding open elevator doors for white men, and being polite and professional to everyone because this is how I expect to be treated. Treating others with respect is what I consider a job that earns you the right to be respected by others. I'm no angel, but I felt that I had earned that respect. I evaluated myself. I was an educated, well-dressed, nonviolent, tax-paying, respectful citizen minding my own business. I have gained my boots and my straps through education, hard work, and the sacrifices of those who came before me, and all of that by the grace of God. Yet despite all of this, I got torn down in public in the middle of a downtown main street by some yahoo who obviously feels that no matter what I as an American Negro do, no matter what I achieve, bootstraps and all, I am still a nigger to him. This is our challenge: to be better than that. It's about the ability to control our anger and make wise choices instead of reacting to the ignorance that has long been draped over the painful faces of American Negroes. After a moment of thought about this situation, it made me more determined and more confident in my abilities to face the hurdles of life and go on. Dramatic? Indeed. It also showed me how much more of a man I was than that person that shouted the obscenity at me. But there was one thing about that incident that bothers me even to this day. It was the fact that when this white guy rolled down his window to belittle me, I saw what looked like his teenaged son in the passenger seat. A transfer of ignorance? Maybe. Hopefully he is a new generation of people who will have the guts to resist the negative teachings and upbringing of his father, and he will make wiser choices. I have always believed that while our children are our future, parents are our today. You can't see tomorrow until you get past today. So where is the problem? It does no good to have boots and straps if you are still treated as though you're barefoot. It's not enough to have boots and straps. I'd rather be barefooted and treated with decency and respect than to have poured out half of my life only to be ignored and disrespected.

In spite of it all, we have endured and will continue to endure. Where respect is earned, respect must be returned. My situation is one that is played out in every city in America, every day, amongst different races. By no means is it an isolated incident. My point in all of this is not to produce anger or hostility because this is not an indictment on all white people or any people for that matter, knowing that we are more cruel to ourselves as American Negroes than any other race could be to us, but to point out the fact that boots and straps are not to be looked at as tangible items but a mental conditioning. Being called a nigger does not in and of itself bother me. It is a fortunate fact in this country that there is such a thing as free speech, and being a racist is not illegal. However, I don't believe that the creators of this privilege intended it to be abused, even though there is very little that can be thought of that was meant to be good that was not abused in some way. A man by the name of Voltaire said, "I may not like what you say, but I'll fight to the death your right to say it."

Unfortunately, the same applies today. Man has discovered, not created, all kinds of life-saving medicinal drugs that other men have found ways to abuse. Airplanes that allow people all over the world the luxury of comfortable travel are now being flown into buildings or used to transport drugs to communities all over the world. Police and authorities set up to protect those communities often times succumb to the temptations of those against whom they are suppose to protect. The pleasures of marital lovemaking are now a way to generate income. The true meaning of marriage is distorted. And we have our own little convenient reasons for them all. But we do have the right to do most anything or say most anything. Our legal system can pass laws as quickly as we can think of other unthinkable things to do, like legalizing certain drugs. We as American Negroes are the last people to fight against rights. However, we know how devastating the abuse of rights can be. Those who have not felt the sting of it generations past and present can only think of new ways to abuse those rights. To see just how much they can fit under that umbrella of acceptance. The problem with that is that the more you put under that umbrella the more something has to be pushed out. And that's where we come in—or are pushed out—we being shut-out blacks, poor whites, children, and anyone with any hint of religious dignity and old-fashioned morals.

Another reason why the word nigger does not provoke me as much—and I'd be a liar unless I used *as much*, only because I'm intelligent—is because it is used as a weapon mostly in the hands—or mouths I should say—of our accusers. A weapon used to validate the myths and lies created by our accusers. And like magic dust, we succumb to its powers. Blacks now use it more than white people do on ourselves. This weapon is designed to produce anger, yet black people have managed to de-fang it down to a term of endearment. The devil's main and most effective weapon is to make us believe that he doesn't exist. That turns people toward another target. Each other. It couldn't have been one who *does* exist. Existence is validated by tangibility in the mind of those so insecure with themselves that they must have a target to shoot at, an enemy to blame, a nigger. Faith is an intangible reality. But you can't lay your hands on that, so it doesn't exist either, again, to the unsecure, which brings me to my point. If a man aims a gun at me that I gave him and validated for him, and I know that it has blanks in it, why should I flinch, unless I don't trust myself? It makes a lot of noise, but the noise, soon and as suddenly as it came, goes away. Now, once again, it comes back to where we started, me and you, the real problem. How long must I load your gun and flinch? That is the question. The existence of the weapon makes me flinch, but faith allows me to stand still (or walk away). Every time I flinch, I throw off positive anger, positive energy that flows to my enemy. This is what sustains his or her existence. Their anger and mistreatment and oppression are not geared toward making us weak but to make them strong, and the one thing I have to understand is the reality of this. Mentally, this is very destructive to one's net worth as a human being.

There has always been talk of legalizing drugs in order to take the power out of it—that power and drive being money. Take the profit out of it, and you take the demand out of it is what is expected. To me, it's like offering an alcoholic a free tab at the bar so that he won't spend all of his money on alcohol. The biggest problem with that theory is that while you may take the demand out of it, you don't take the need—or dependency it creates—out of it. The more potent drugs, such as crack cocaine, have been fairly equally distributed among races, according to latest statistics. An abnormally higher percentage of those in jail for the use of drugs are black! According to NCBI (National Center for Biotechnology Information, US Library of Medicine Public Access), 82 percent of blacks reported current cocaine use compared to 54 percent of Hispanics and 57 percent of whites. I call it the Self-Destruction Theory.

But the theory can be used in the case of the dreaded N word. Take the fear out of that loud noise, and you will take back your positive energy. The reason nonviolence was such an effective weapon insisted upon by Dr. King was because it was a known fact, and still is today, that you cannot forcefully change another person's mind. He or she must come to his or her own reality. The only way a man can truly know how bad his dog is is when his dog turns on his master. I'm not advocating not protecting yourself, nor am I promoting violence. I am saying that the anger you show only proves that the weapon selected to use on you is working. Use it as long as it works. You have boots. You have straps. You can either use them to take you great places or waste your time kicking at some fool's dog because he called you a reflection of himself, nigger. And to show you how much we believe him, we have now reserved the right for blacks to call each other nigger(s). Somehow it's different? Do we hate ourselves that much? Nigger in any language, coming out of the mouth of a person of any color, anywhere—hood included—means the same derogatory and devastating thing and is unacceptable. However, any brother that calls me that is still my brother. He is just very confused, lost, and trapped in a world he didn't create but one he chooses to dwell in, and he needs help getting out. Let him know you don't like it or its history and tell him/her not to call you that again. It won't be easy. We've got some bad dogs too. But for the grace of God.

No Parking

One evening while I was downtown on business, I parked in front of the bank that I was going to. The curb was one where delivery drivers normally parked, and though there was not a No Parking sign there, there was painted on the curb the words No Standing. Because I was on a business call there at the bank, I parked there. I was there for about fifteen minutes, and when I returned, I had been slapped with a "no parking" ticket. Now normally I would simply face the facts and take or mail in the money, but considering my financial situation at the time, I decided to opt for the meeting with the official to plead my case and try to get the ticket dropped.

Well, my scheduled date was set. I went into the city official's office. He was an older, white-haired, stern, business, professional type. His desk had a nameplate on one side, and on the other side of the office was a large table with a chair on either end. I felt as if I had used up all appeals and was being escorted to my last sit down. He, without discussion, showed me to my seat on one end of the large, wood-grained, smooth, latex-coated table, adjusted a microphone on the table in front of me, and told me to speak into the microphone. No chitchat. No "How was your day?" Just business as usual. He then informed me that this meeting would be taped and for me to state my name and reason for coming. I did so and explained to him that there was only a No Standing sign painted on the curb, but if *that* was illegal, then I'm not guilty of the *parking* violation. I then told him that what I really came to do was to ask that the ticket be dropped this time because twenty dollars for a fifteen-minute parking violation would be tough on me right now, being a single parent and doing the best that I could to raise a child and make ends meet. I told him that I would not argue the violation. I was simply asking for a warning this time, as it is probably done every day in every city across this country (though I didn't put it quite that bluntly). I was as open and honest as I always try to be because I figured that it was the right thing to do.

He allowed me to finish my plea without a word, and his expression did not change much. It was as if he just wanted me to hurry up so that he could get back to what he was doing or to get to the next victim. When I finished, he concluded the taping, turned off the microphone, proceeded to write out my ticket, and told me that I had committed a parking violation and for me to pay the lady out front. Period. Now, what did I expect? I expected to get credit for my honesty. Even if I still had to pay the ticket, I at least expected or hoped for a comment like, "Mr. Walker, I admire your honesty, and I would hope you continue to stay honest. I sympathize with your struggle to raise a child alone and the road that you may be traveling in doing so. I admire and respect that. However, the law is plain, and if I allow it to be circumvented by emotional circumstances, I wouldn't be doing my job and a lot of people would be unemployed. Even though I cannot dismiss this ticket, I would like to encourage you to continue to be honest and responsible." Am I dreaming?

I honestly did hope for a more positive response similar to that, because as I walked out of that building, I thought to myself, *Next time I'll lie and say that there was no sign, nor was the officer justified in giving me that ticket. It's my word against his and a waste of the taxpayer's money by appealing this for as long as it takes to get it dropped. I was guilty the minute I walked through the door of that office. Honesty doesn't seem to get people as far as dishonesty, it seems. You get no credit for being honest, and nowadays compassion is only uttered at the butt of a joke. Thanks for the encouragement, buddy!* I shall press on, in honesty, regardless. Because I know that it's not the way things are, but the way some people are, and if I allow myself to be dictated by the number of—however many—uncaring people out there, I might end up just like them. This world needs encouragement, not pessimism and hatred. This is why our children, black, white, and all that fall in between, are as insensitive and as hardcore as they are. This man was a parent, a grandfather most likely, and a figurehead for someone much like the guy who shouted obscenities at me as I crossed the street with his son in the van next to him. I'm no angel, but for the grace of God.

Expression Four

BOOTSTRAPS 101

Thou Shall Strike Thy Neighbor

Power can be defined in as many ways as it can be delivered. Force defines the persuasiveness of power. Reality is power's due diligence. And what thoughts are conjured up in the mind of the masses when the phrase *strike a blow* is uttered in the path of anger? Power cannot stand alone. It must be accompanied by its relative efforts to be effective. Power is an act of unity.

Unity, however, is like a river. It can be pristine, forever moving, flowing as if it had a purpose, as it usually does. It is fine as long as it stays within it banks. But like those whose purpose deviates, there will always be some who will flow outside of its banks and go crashing against the rocks. Outside of its element, this serene river becomes a dangerous menace to whomever or whatever gets in its way.

Yet power and unity must go hand in hand to be truly effective. Too much of either can cause you to lose focus. And though unity is power, power does not beget unity.

The key here is unity. Unity—not for the sake of separatism but for the sake of progress, respect, and brotherhood. Why do we as American Negroes hate each other so much? Why do we as American Negroes distrust one another so much? Why do we have such a problem working together for the sake of our future and for the sake of progress within? Are we in a dash that pits each person against the other, or are we in a marathon that almost requires unity and causes everyone to pat one another on the back and wish them well even though we are competing with each other? However, when you look at that marathon, there is some of everyone. Black, white, Chinese, Japanese, Hispanic. It's sort of like the way Malcolm X Little reacted when he took his first trip to Mecca and noticed white Muslims and others who were Muslims as well as himself. He thought about the fact that he was fighting against people, some of whom were walking in the same direction as he was. He then refocused on the fact that all whites weren't enemies, just the bad ones. The same can be said about the American Negro or any other *different* person in this world of ours.

But why is it that other foreigners and immigrants can come to this country and almost immediately succeed—go into business, become self-sufficient and successful—and we as American Negroes, who have been in this country long enough to grow some pretty effective roots of our own, do not own significant businesses in our own neighborhoods or on Main Street for that fact? One of the most powerful tools we have is our voice. Yes, a mind is a terrible thing to waste, and an education is imperative, but it doesn't take an education to know when you've been done wrong or that you're still on the bottom talking about what you could've or should've done. It may take an educated mind to get you out, but it doesn't take much thinking to see that you're in hole. Individually or united, we can be effectual.

One day several years ago, I went to a small store in my neighborhood. It was a converted 7-Eleven that was taken over by foreigners who were very suspect of American Negroes in their store. Now I certainly have nothing against anyone who shops, sells, opens, or runs a business anywhere they please. We are afforded that same privilege. But on this particular evening, I dashed in to pick up an item. I stood in line with the rest of the folks there, and when I got up to the counter to pay for my items, I handed the attendant—who, by the way, was in training with his coach standing by—a twenty-dollar bill for an item that cost a dollar and some change. The attendant gave me change back as though I had given him a five-dollar bill instead of a twenty. I respectfully told him that

I had given him a twenty-dollar bill. He said I did not. I assured him that I did, and I know I did because at the time, that was all of the money I had in my wallet, and being a single parent with a five-year-old daughter to take care of, I needed my money. We went back and forth a couple of times, and the people in line behind me were waiting on this misunderstanding to end. Then the white man behind me in line told the attendant that I did indeed give him a twenty-dollar bill because he saw me give it to him. Now I had never seen or met this man in my life, but the attendant then suggested that the white man and I were working together in some scheme to pull this trick on him, and he again refused to correct my change. He suggested that I wait until the next morning when they would do a shift change and count the money, and if it showed the register as being over, he'd give me my money, or I could speak to his manager who, by the way, would not be in until the following day. People in line were getting upset, and the line was getting quite long. It was about six at night, and most, like myself, had just gotten off from work and went into the store to grab a little something on the way home, hoping to get out fast. Thinking about that, and being one who was agreeable to inconvenience, I said okay and left the store.

The drive home was short but very long that evening, which had now turned to night. And I decided on the way home that tonight I would make a change and not be so agreeable with someone else's mistake. Besides that, I needed my money. So, I went home, changed into some sweats and tennis shoes, went up to the nearest five-and-dime store, and bought some large poster boards. I then went back to the house and nailed some wooden sticks to them, drove back down to that store, and my five-year-old daughter and I executed our own strike! My daughter (in my arms) and I picketed that store till the wee hours of the night, holding up signs that talked about the mistrust and dishonesty I was dealt without the slightest benefit of the doubt given me. The attendant came out later that night and threatened to call the police. I stayed. So the store called the police on me, and they came out, and knowing that this was public property, they could only tell me not to park my car directly in front of the store and not to impede the flow of traffic. Other than that, there was nothing they could do to stop me. So with my daughter, I picketed on because I was causing a lot of people to back up and leave the store. They lost a lot of business that night. I was very surprised also that so many American Negroes came to us, telling me stories of mistreatment that they suffered while in that store and how they were always viewed as suspect and how the store would not allow their children to go into the store for fear of them stealing. I was also approached by some brothers who asked if I needed some help—if you know what I mean—and they were very serious. I told them thanks but no thanks because I didn't want this to turn into a violent confrontation. So they gave me their phone numbers, and said, "Just call."

I was very proud of my five-year-old who walked that line with me, not knowing what was going on or why people kept turning away from the store. She only trusted Daddy. Some people probably looked at me badly for having her out there, but she was a part of me and the main reason for my doing this. Besides, I certainly wasn't going to put her in harm's way. Later that night, close to midnight, the trainee's attendant came out, never admitting to a mistake, and offered me my money back. But this was not a sincere gesture. It was only because I was affecting their bottom line. At this point, it became another issue. Trust. I didn't want handouts. I wanted what was rightfully mine. My honesty was in question now and also how this was handled by the store. Well, to make a long story short, I got my money and learned a very good and important lesson to boot. One (and a half) can make a difference. Just imagine what unity can do.

Not unity for the sake of getting together or for violence but for the sake of progress and showing that a difference can be made if done for the right reasons and with respect and dignity and tact and for a purpose that expands beyond yourself. Sometimes it's okay to *strike* your neighbor.

Go to Hell!

One day I was in a church back home, and the preacher told the congregation about an incident that happened to him just the week before. He said his brother-in-law called him and asked him for a small loan to hold him over for a while. Being the preacher that he was and knowing his brother-in-law the way he did, he asked him a question. The question was, "What has God done for you lately?" The brother-in-law, not being the most responsible man in the world, not to mention married and unemployed, said, "Nothin'!"

"Nothing?" the preacher repeated.

"Nothin'!" repeated the brother-in-law.

"You mean God has never done *anything* for you? Nothing?" the preacher asked.

"No, God hasn't done nothin' for me. Look at me," he said. "I ain't got no job. My wife and I ain't getting along; she's always on my back. I got no peace in my own home. I got no money. I'm just sick and tired. Does it look like God's done *anything* for me?"

"Well," the preacher got into his sermon mode now, "did you get up this morning?"

"Yeah," said the brother-in-law.

"Are you still breathing?" said the preacher.

"Barely," said the brother-in-law.

"You got clothes on your back?" said the preacher.

"Yeah."

"Have you eaten anything today?"

"Yea, I ate something today."

"Now, you've done all of that, and you still say God has done *nothing* for you?"

"I'm still not happy. I'm still miserable. No. No, God ain't done nothin' for me!" said the brother-in-law.

"Well," the preacher said, rather disturbed, "since you still say God has done *nothing* for you, by the power vested in me by God as a preacher of the Gospel of Jesus Christ, and since you say that God has done nothing for you, I declare by the powers vested in me that you go to hell! If God has ignored you that much, then it's obvious to me that that's where you're going." The preacher denied his loan, figuring it to be throwing good money after bad and hung up the phone.

Have you ever felt like telling someone that? In the proper context of course. Especially people who have more than they appreciate. Those who seem to simply meander through life, taking life for granted. Those who seem to show no value for life. Those who seem to have no recollection of their past, and their future ends at the tip of their nose. They are indeed dangerous people because if you don't hold much value for your own life, how much will you have for others? It seems very evident that the American Negro, certainly not all but enough to cause great harm, has a problem with self-identification and self-acceptance. We don't love one another. With the way we drug, maim, disrespect, and kill each other, we seem to devalue our very existence. We have a unique ability to live up to what the Native American Indians call the *dominant white man's* views.

Now, there's a good part of the American Negro population who, when they read this, will be absolutely appalled at the fact that I could think this, let alone write it. But on the other side of the fence, there are just as many American Negroes who are applauding what they've come to know as the truth, and whichever side of the fence you are on will determine how long we will be in this state of affairs. Whether or not there is a right or wrong side of this fence, there does seem to be a chasm between us, and that chasm to many is known as hell. We're not followed around in department and grocery stores for nothing. Life is usually based on a pattern. A pattern we did not create but continue to validate, that we may make life manageable and predictable for the sake of order. "This is who they say that I am, so that's what I'll be." We have created a pattern of behavior that indicts us all. Lack of parental control. Lack of creating a vision for our children. Lack of family values. Lack of family loyalty. Lack of confidence not only for our people but also for us individually. Lack of faith and trust in the same God that brought us out of our Egypt.

Sure, these statements can be applied to others as well, but we are first—though not only—responsible for ourselves. We have caused ourselves to become suspect though we did not create this suspicion. And only we can destroy that reputation. An extremely difficult task indeed because it requires changing the minds of people, starting with ourselves. Facing ourselves is much more difficult than facing others. Just another strap in the boot of life.

Stop Kicking Your Own Ass

The Enemy

There was a time when we knew who the enemy was. It had flesh and blood and a face, and when its arms went up to strike you, you could see the veins in its neck and its clenched teeth straining to gather all of the power it could muster to strike a blow against its target. And its target was usually you. Its target was usually black. But was that the real enemy? And was the target really aimed at black people? Or was it simply aimed at blackness. Blackness has been infiltrated into the minds of many as fear. Could it have been fear striking at fear? Though the enemy is not known to fight against itself, it is afraid of the very weapon it uses to protect itself. Therefore, it feels that in order to survive, it must destroy that which it fears the most, or at the very least control it.

The Word that black people relied on for centuries—the Bible or Good Book, as it is affectionately called—says in Ephesians 6:12 that our (true) struggle is not—was not, will not, and never will be—against flesh and blood but against the rulers, against the powers, against the world forces of this darkness, against the spiritual forces of wickedness in the heavenly places. Do we not know who the enemy is? Would we recognize the enemy if we saw it or him or her or them?

In the Bible, in the book of Numbers 22:22, there is a most unusual but thought-provoking story about such an enemy. The cause of the debate was because Balak, the king of Moab, sent word to a man called Balaam to curse the people who came out of Egypt because there were so many of them that they "covered the surface of the land" as they exited Egypt, and there were too many for him to defeat. So now the enemy is afraid of the very weapon it used to protect itself. These people were slaves of pharaoh. God got angry at Balaam because he was going. He was riding on his donkey (or ass) with his two servants when the angel of the Lord took his stand in the middle of the road as adversary against him. Balaam couldn't see the angel with sword drawn to kill him, but his ass could. So the ass turned in another direction into a field. Balaam, surprised at the ass's sudden move, kicked his own ass to get her back onto the pathway. But up the path a little ways, the angel showed up again in the middle of the narrow road, with sword drawn to kill Balaam for not following the command of God and following instead the command of a man, Balak, who was the king of Moab. Only this time there was a wall on both sides of the road. So the ass, in an attempt to ease by the angel, slid up as close to the wall as she could, pressing Balaam's foot against the wall. Again Balaam struck the ass. A short distance up the road, the angel appeared once again in the middle of the road, and there was nowhere to turn left or right and no room to squeeze by the angel, so the ass just laid laid down. Now I can just imagine what was going on in the mind of the ass, but can you imagine what Balaam was thinking?, And what do you think he did? He got off of the ass and struck her with his stick again. It was at that time the Lord opened the mouth of the ass and gave it the ability to speak. Now I can think of some choice words to say to Balaam had I been in that situation, but the ass said to Balaam, "What have I done to you that you have struck me these three times?"

The thing that surprises me is that Balaam just simply answered the ass back, saying that she had made him look bad and that if he had had a sword in his hand instead of a stick, he would have killed her by now. The ass then asked Balaam if the behavior he witnessed from her was something that he had ever witnessed her do in the time they had been together, to which Balaam answered, "No." It was at that time the Lord opened the eyes of Balaam, and he saw the angel of the Lord standing there, sword drawn. And the Lord explained to Balaam that had it not been for the ass, he would have surely been dead now. What we see and what we *perceive* to see oftentimes can be totally different. The real enemy is many times unseen, so we strike out at the tools that he uses to fulfill its mission. Tools are usually disposable. Therefore, they have no real value in the particular mission except to deceive you. While we are fighting against flesh and blood—people who are perceived to be our enemy, those whose backs we are riding—they are trying to protect us and tell us who the real enemy is. You can't see him or touch him.

You can't see the veins well up in his neck as he raises his hand to strike you. Therefore, could it be that because of that, we strike out at that which is nearest to us? Us! Have we been deceived? Are we deceiving ourselves because of how we think of one another? Have we been told by others who we are for so long that we now believe it, even to the point of distrusting those American Negroes—and concerned whites and others—who try to convince us otherwise?

Many may think that I or others who speak as I do are too black oriented and always crying about the plight of black people when God says to love your brother, etc. … I understand that. But I also understand that we need to face the fact that we are different. You can run from that until you drop of sheer exhaustion, but our history is different from—not necessarily more important than—any other race on the face of the earth. I'm sure I've said it once, and I'll say it a thousand times more: in order to correct a bad chair, you must correct the bad leg on the chair, not talk about how good the other three are. Nor should you balance yourself on the remaining three for support, but instead address the real problem. Do not talk about how good the seat part of the chair is and how we should be thankful for that, but instead address the problem. For any entity to succeed, you must put your efforts on the problem. Fix the problem and improve everyone. You can't fix it by ignoring it or convincing yourself that it does not deserve as much attention as anything else. This is not a popularity contest. This is not about protecting your precious reputations. This is not about bruising your fragile ego. This is more important than what people might say about you. This is not about focusing on those three stable legs because it's your bread and butter, so you'll throw out some crumbs to and make your living off of the broken leg. It's about facing the fact that you are not always right, and other people might have opinions of their own that are just as important. History has shown that *that* is usually where the solutions come from. You think! So let's talk about solutions.

Expression Five

SOLUTIONS

Pass it off?

Run away?

Duke it out?

Work it out.

Strengths

Weaknesses

Solutions

Our Strengths

Our Strengths and Struggles
Past and Present

I don't think that one can talk about strengths without talking about both past and present struggles, because they are forever linked. One feeds off of the other. It is ultimately our past that makes our present strong.

One day I went to see a man I highly respect, to pick his brain and ask for his advice in helping out a mutual acquaintance of ours who had been, in effect, blindfolded and led to and dropped into a proverbial hole with promises that were never, and were never meant to be, kept by people whose aim seemingly was to send a message to the rest of us American Negroes about just who was in control. We met for a good while, discussing all angles of the situation and trying to figure out who in other places and strategic positions—otherwise known as networking as opposed to neck-working—within the organization we could call on to help put our strategy together in a peaceful and legal manner. While we were calling out some names—black, white, or otherwise—my mentor said something that only experience could have realized. He said that no color or race is without the potential to burn you, but even with that, who one selects to help will depend not on where they are in hierarchy but more importantly how they got there, in most cases. In other words, whatever it took for them to get to where they are will be the same thing we'll have to depend on as help from them. If they were handed their position by simply being cooperative with the status quo, they will continue to be loyal to the hand that feeds them to avoid losing what they have or to get further in their own aspirations. On the other hand, if there was unfair resistance and fight and a struggle to claim what was earned, then that's what they are accustomed to doing, and that's what they'll do for you. Now realizing that there are no absolutes to this train of thought, I daresay that the percentages will speak very loudly for themselves, and in sensitive situations like we were discussing, one cannot ignore the percentages.

The key word I want to put a tag on here is *struggle*. The struggle. Our struggle is our strength. Struggle is what causes you to fight so hard for your future because you appreciate your past. You respect your past. I have to put it that way to separate out those who selfishly step on others—greed—to stay ahead for their own aggrandizement. However, moving ahead is much like planning to take a trip. A one-way trip, if you're not planning on going back. But planning to go from point A to point B must depend on your knowing first where point A is. You cannot draw a line from nothing to something because you'll never know whether the point you are on is where you started from or where you've ended up.

We all know the story about the butterfly and the cocoon. There was once a boy who saw a butterfly struggling to get out of its cocoon, and feeling pity for it, he helped the moth tear open the cocoon. The moth dropped to the ground and died. The boy later learned that the struggle was a natural part of the survival of the moth, which, by the time it ran its natural course to get out of the cocoon, was to be a beautiful butterfly with a future. Well, whether or not we as a black people were meant to go through what we have—and are still going through—we certainly can't deny the truth any more than we can negate our past. The struggle is not our enemy; it is our strength. But we treat it like an albatross, a weight forever on our backs. Like slavery. A struggle was not made to dwell in; it was made to climb out of. Too many of us are still wallowing in the mud pits of struggle. Fight through it, grow strong from it, and show yourself worthy of it, but in the name of Jesus, get out of it! Even Jesus had to carry a cross. And though it was the cross that saved us, His intent was not for us to climb up there with Him but for Him to come down to show us how to overcome challenges. He was taken down off of that cross, but what He used as strength and evidence of love to all people were His scars. Too many of us are still hanging on that cross. Our struggle is in what got us up there. The power that got us down was our faith and strength. But it was love that got Jesus off of that cross.

Struggle creates power, and that power is love. The toughest struggle we as a black people have now is loving ourselves first—then one another, then others. Why is it that we only band together in the midst of adversity? We call each other names not because we hate one another but because we hate ourselves. We have made ourselves to look like the creators of racial profiling. We treat one another the way others say that we are. Who knows us better than we do? We've started believing all of the negative things said about us, so we pass the hurt on to another one of our own. We as a people have been hurt deeply and are now simply asked to let it go. That's easier said than done, but for the sake of our future, we must. But how can we when we are reminded of it over and over and over again each day? Regardless, we must. Stop perpetuating the struggle. Use it. Let's start by convincing ourselves that we are worth something. Confess it and believe it. I am not a nigger. It's Negro, please. I am *not* a nigger. I am *not* a nigger. I am struggle. I am a child of God. For many American Negroes, that is a hard statement to make and an even harder one to believe. I mean *truly* believe. Our actions convict us. Now I can move. Now I can move on.

Our Faith

Martin Luther King Jr. is to the younger generations what Jesus is to many people today. He was just a nice man who tried to help and got killed for it.

And that frightens us!

We kill each other every day for nothing.

Are you not willing to die for something?

Where faith ends, trust must begin. For the amount of your trust will determine your increase in faith.

Faith is many things to many people, but its true author is God. I believe that the most powerful force on earth—that man has to battle always—is temptation. The one thing that can defeat it hands down is faith. But faith alone is not the thing that helps you. It's much like love. Love was meant to be shared or given away. To have it and not share it makes it useless. Faith is given to be filled and fulfilled. It reminds me of how God provided manna or flakes from heaven to feed the children of Israel in the desert. He told them that when it came down, they could get all that they could eat, but only for each day alone. If they stored up some for the next day, it would spoil, as one family found out. That's the way faith is. It must be used as needed, daily. It may not spoil, but it becomes just as useless as the flakes if not used when needed. It's a jar that must be filled; otherwise it is just a jar not being used for its purpose. But the thing that you must remember is that temptation is forever and faith is not a one-shot thing. Faith is like Moses raising his hand (or staff) on the hill during battle, and as long as his hand is raised, his people are winning the battle, but sometimes you just get tired. And temptation is waiting for an opening for you to put your hand down. When you realize it, you quickly put your hand up again, but each time you lower your hand, temptation gets a stronger foothold. It's the same way with American Negroes. There's no need in my going back into slavery, civil rights, inequalities, and the like. We've heard all of that before, and we know about all of that. We've battled our way through so much. By faith. Faith says, "I don't know what's up ahead, but I know I've gotta go there because I know I can't stay here."

There is no true faith without God. Period. Whatever manner of faith you have, God has got to be in it somewhere, or it is not faith; it's chance, or "I think," or even worse, luck. Faith is bigger than we are. Faith helps us forgive ourselves even when others won't. Faith makes us believe in spite of. And most importantly, faith is all-inclusive. It's the bridge that allows us to go from tolerating to loving. Dr. Tony Evans once said that "faith is the bridge that connects the natural with the supernatural." Everyone has faith, but many substitute it with money, clout, privilege, or power, and if faith is something you put your trust in, it should be something that will outlast critical times.

So why all of this talk about faith and God? Because there is so much similarity in the plight of the children of Israel as described in the Bible and the African and American Negro. It was faith that brought the children of Israel out of bondage and to a land of opportunity. However, after freedom came the wilderness as it was for black slaves and black Americans. Faith, strength, and God are so intertwined that there is no strength without faith and no faith without God. Have we abandoned our first love? Is it no longer the in thing to love, worship, praise, and yes—even need God? I think it is more the problem of lowering God from *needed* to *as needed*. When we raise God from *as needed* to *needed,* we will see our lives change as a people, as a nation, and as a world. We cannot leave God out. That is impossible. We must maintain faith. It is our most powerful strength. Faith gives us the courage to press on.

Do we need faith to see to it that we will overcome? No. To say that we will overcome puts the burden on us. That's a heavy burden. Besides, overcome what? The Bible says that our struggle is not against flesh and blood but against the rulers, against the powers, against the world forces, and against the spiritual forces of wickedness in the heavenly places. And how will we know when we've overcome? Many would not know overcome if we stepped in it. Give that burden to God. He's in heavenly places. But does that mean we pray to God and simply walk away? No. Just as the slaves would sing while they were burdened down, so must we pray while we work. Faith is not a magic carpet ride. You must still work hard to achieve anything. Faith gives you the strength, fortitude, persistence, protection, reason, and vision, but you must still work hard to validate it. Salvation is free. Everything else, we work for.

Three things we must do:

- understand what true success is
- embrace and face fear
- understand the power of delayed gratification

In the words of Reverend John Hagee: "You were born an original! Don't you dare die a cheap copy of someone else!"

Our Weaknesses

Not Passing on the Past
We Give Our Children More Future than Past

I'm reminded of the fact that more and more of our youth are encouraged to leave school early when enticed by the lure of money and fame by sports franchises. Some are recruited straight out of high school and never enter the college they would have indeed been fortunate to attend. But this is being done at the encouragement of the parents for their children to grab more future than past. I certainly don't expect parents to turn down once-in-a-lifetime opportunities, though there are certainly times when even that is the more appropriate thing to do. But I'm also certainly not saying that we should consider that their future. A future based on money. It's a shame that we've condensed the word future to money. Now, I'm sure that there are many who are snarling up their noses at this last statement of mine, saying that I would probably do the same were I or a child of mine were in similar circumstances, or even that I'm saying this because I may not have a child in that position, and that jealousy has reared its ugly head. If that's what you're saying, you've missed my point totally. People say that money does not bring happiness. These people are getting happiness mixed up with joy. Money can bring happiness, but happiness is finite. It's not how much money we make but how wisely we use that money, and that takes knowledge. In other words, it's not how much money that comes out of your pocket as effort, but how much comes back in as results. That is the ultimate goal.

Success without morals is dangerous to any person. It's like a loaded gun in the hands of a baby. I wish our children all of the success in the world but not at the expense of their morality, dignity, humanity, and ignoring their past. Our youth do not know about their past because we as parents, grandparents, and other relatives and friends fail to remind them or tell them. Many parents cannot get past the anger of their past themselves and as a result transfer it to generations of tolerant kids who think that their present is their past. I take you again to the children of Israel in the Bible. Remember, they were set free and headed to the Promised Land. A land of milk and honey. Milk and honey were representative of success and happiness prepared by someone else. They were on their way to reap the benefits of the labors of others who did not appreciate from where their blessings came. They were being led to take over the blessings of other people's hard work because those people, though wildly successful in their own right, forgot from whom their blessings came. They forgot their past or simply ignored it and considered each day as their own private past. But the one thing that stands out in my mind about that forty-year trip going around in circles was a couple of statements made by God before that trip to success got started.

First was in Exodus 13:17, where God basically said that He was not going to lead His people to their success by the quickest or easiest route, "Lest the people change their minds when they see war, and they return to Egypt." If we learn from our past, we'll see that success is never easy, only because many of us simply can't handle it, and we go back to the way we feel most comfortable. For many, that's a pig going back to wallow in the mud with a diamond in his nose. But another very important statement was when God told the fathers to tell their sons from where they came from and that "It is because of what the Lord did for me when I came out of Egypt." In other words, never forget your past; it is the key to your future. Our children do not know their past but are pushed towards what is told to them to be a better future. Even though we now live in an age of superior technology and access to information, they are not being encouraged or inspired enough to get them to see where they came from, so they do not appreciate what they already have or whose shoulders their generation has stood on to allow them their future. Remembering our past is very important to our future. I don't mean dwell in the past or stay angry about it. Nor do I mean seeing us as some superior race. Just know it. Remember it. Use it as a catalyst to propel you into a land of milk and honey. And when you get there, you'll appreciate it first and enjoy it more.

Tolerating Our Imperfections

One thing that bothers black people more than many things is bad customer service from us to us. Whether ordering fries at a fast-food restaurant or buying clothes from a department store, when you encounter black folk, you usually get subpar service for your hard-earned buck. This is certainly not a blanket statement inclusive of all black folk. There are many who are very well rounded, respectful, and professional. It seems we don't run into them much. All it takes is one bad black customer service experience, and we turn into white folks. We are very hard on ourselves. We are judged by many whites as uneducated and without the capacity to think and be courteous at the same time. Oh, many won't say that to your face but certainly think it. We, all too often, live up to that. But the thing that bothers me is that we, black folks, tolerate it. If a black person acts professionally, they are branded white. Sometimes you can't win for losing. Most times we simply tolerate it. Why is that?

The funny thing is that when I talk to black folk one on one, they agree with me, but publicly I'm just another brother *low rating* black folk. Now, I'll talk about white folk as needed. That makes me bad and *un-Christian-like*. When I talk about black folk, that makes me part of the black problem of 'diss'-unity. We are a country of people quick to talk about others without dealing with ourselves. There is a problem in black America. Like it or not, don't shoot the messenger. And the only way to solve it is to first talk about it. Huddle up, black folks!

I've noticed, and many others have who have the guts to admit it, that northern black people are different from southern black people. I don't necessarily mean geographically throughout the country. I mean within city-to-city boundaries, northern representing the affluent areas in a city, and southern representing the less affluent to poor areas of a city. For example, if a reputable black food establishment were to open up in the southern area of a city, it oftentimes has a less attractive setting or environment. Poorly paved parking areas, unmatched tables and chairs, trophies along the walls, makeshift serving areas, and overall not much thought put into planning for a nice eating environment. Now, we'll certainly lay the blame on the lack of or inability to get adequate financing, and that may indeed play a part. But I guarantee you that if that same black owner were to open up another restaurant in the northern sector, much more thought would go into comfort, environment, feel, neatness, and ambiance. And it would be less about finance and more about expectation.

That's right, expectation. Expectation is a big reason why more attention to details would be put into that particular project. You see, black people know that white people expect more of themselves, their surroundings, and living conditions, and because we know that, we adapt to that based on their expectations. We rise to a higher level of expectation when we deal with white people than with ourselves. Why? Because we allow our own expectations to be lowered when we are around one another's environment, and the worst thing about that is that we tolerate it. We blame it on that myth that when we are around our own people, we should act like we are expected to act—talk a different way, handle our business in a different way, and create an environment that is comfortable (as opposed to professional) to us. Well, I'm not comfortable with a restaurant with potholes in the parking lot, nine different color chairs to sit on, a server who wears everything he's serving today on his apron with no sanitary gloves on and answering me with words like "Huh?" instead of "Excuse me?" and "Yo, chief, what's it gon' be?" instead of "May I help you?" and "All right" instead of "Thank you." Don't get me wrong; there are places for that and without embarrassment or apologies to anyone. But let's be professional when the time for professionalism is upon us, not only up north but to ourselves especially.

If you want to show me brotherhood, show me that you can adapt to any situation. Again I say that the main problem is that we tolerate it. Up north, we know that white folk don't tolerate it. And many times it's not because of their misunderstanding or unwillingness to accept our way of life. Sometimes it is. But whether it is or not, we should have enough dignity within ourselves whether north or south to adjust to different environments. Our expectations are too low among ourselves. We as black people tolerate subpar service without correcting it on the spot, and if black folk are working in an establishment that is white owned or a chain store, even *they* lower their expectations of that environment because of how we are known to present ourselves.

Many who read this will accuse me of being around whites too much and as a result having lost my identity. Well, think what you must. I know who I am and where I come from. I live and will die black. I also think highly enough of myself to expect others, black or white, to treat me with respect, especially when I decide to spend my hard-earned money in your establishment. You are doing me no favors. A sandwich from any other place is a sandwich. We must increase the expectations of ourselves and stop tolerating bad service. The problem therein again lies at home first but also in the hands of responsible and professional black men and women to teach our black youth the importance of professionalism. Pull your pants up, take that earring out of your ear, and speak clearly with confidence. Act like you're going to hold office in this land, own a business one day, cure cancer, or just be the best darn mechanic with an equally sterling reputation for as much as fairness, honesty, and an education—whatever level—can buy you. And please understand that I'm not just directing this lack of servant hood to our youth.

We in the black community also have some grown folk that I would never tell my child to respect. Let's first start acting like parents and then take back our families. As ironic as it may sound, many of our youth don't do what you say because you don't say to them what you want them to do.

Imperfection goes far beyond customer service. It infiltrates one's lifestyle. We will never be perfect humans, but that doesn't stop us from striving for it. We must stop tolerating imperfection because indeed what each generation tolerates the next generation will embrace. Black people must not embrace imperfection.

It takes a village? No! It took a village. Let's wake up! There is no more village! We have abandoned the village! There are now strangers in the village! It takes a faith-filled mother and a father to raise a kid. It takes a family.

Our youth must have a dream, but before the dream, they must be inspired. Then they'll need encouragement to succeed at that dream so that that dream can pull them into the future. They need to be exposed to different things and places. But if your youth are listening to and watching you curse, lie, cheat, gamble (lottery), steal, and then go to church each Sunday, praising the Lord, what can you expect from them? If they see you slow down or run through a Stop sign when you drive a car, what can you expect from them? When they see you park in that handicap space with the big blue picture of the wheelchair painted on it while you say to them "I'll just be a moment," which says to them that it's all right to break a legal or moral law as long as it is for just a moment, don't be surprised when their handicap zone turns into a fake handicap sign they use to put on their rearview mirror, and their moment turns into a shopping spree at the grocer or mall. If they see you allowing them to pile into the car without seat belts emphasized, don't be surprised when you get that call that there was a serious accident, and due to the lack of them using seat belts, your child will not be coming home. We must understand that there are consequences to our actions that affect others. Everything that we do matters.

Instead of trying to leave our children the legacy of cars, homes, or money, we should leave them a legacy of courage. It's going to take that to make it in a world where selfishness, disappointment, and greed walk side by side with honesty and giving. Much like that powerful elephant being held down by a meager stake in the ground and a rope, we must claim victory over that stake by realizing that it's all in our minds. We don't have to lose our minds, just change them.

Simple Solutions

The ultimate solution is this: We must take ownership of everything that we do or say. We must, as the Bible says in Leviticus 26:40, "confess their iniquity and the iniquity of their forefathers" on both sides.

To Thine Own Self Be True

Start with yourself. Are you the best you can be— spiritually, physically, mentally, and economically? All of these must be seen as absolute necessities.

Spiritually

I'm not talking about going to church every once in a while, though I'm certainly not saying don't go to church. I feel that we each—and this includes everyone—need more of a personal relationship with Jesus Christ than just being one of a number of people in a church, wondering what all of the excitement is about. Church is a place to go to affirm publicly what you've learned personally with God. When you simply go to church, many times you leave never feeling changed, just entertained. That's because you came with nothing to affirm. When you spend personal, private, quiet time with the Lord, you can be who you really are, say what you really want to say, without feeling like you're being watched or that your faith is being measured by others around you. God wants you to feel comfortable around Him.

Read your Bible. Learn about this faith you believe in. Learn about who you are and who you were meant to be. Empower yourself. Repent. Let the word of God inspire you. Dream. Be who you are destined to be and realize that it can be so. And in reality, for those who don't believe in God, believe in yourself with the understanding that you are all you've got in the end. That doesn't give me comfort, but we are a product of our choices.

But also realize that there are rules and consequences to your actions. Does that sound familiar? That's what you as a parent expect from your children. And for those of you who may not be married or may not have kids, just remember, you are a kid. You are God's child. You can dream too. As a matter of fact, you have more of an opportunity to be all that you can be in the Lord because you have nothing to hold you back. Now that does not mean that those who have a mate or children are being held back. You have added responsibilities and priorities to juggle. You are in life who you were meant to be—tall, short, black, white, or whatever.

It is important to learn to live life like a child. Children live life for the moment. The only thing that counts to a child is right now. There is no future beyond right now. The only difference is that they really believe that. We know better, but that should not stop us from taking in every moment of each day that God gives us, moment by moment. And if you are one of those who doesn't believe that there is a God, my advice to you is to wake up! God will be God whether you believe in Him or not. Fact of the matter is that every human being has knowledge of God in his or her spirit. The rest is your choice. Not fate.

Physically:
Two-Piece and a Pepper Living

What good are you to you if you don't care enough about yourself to take care of yourself? Specifically speaking, black people are dying by the thousands because of poor eating habits and little to no consistent exercise. High blood pressure, heart attacks, early stages of arthritis, high cholesterol, and just plain, old fat, overweight, obesity—call it whatever makes you feel comfortable—pleasantly plump, full figured, chunky—it all comes down to fat. Lazy could be thrown in there as well. Being physically out of shape affects many parts of your life, as well as relationships and marriage. Being too tired to go to your child's functions, too tired to go to school and get that degree you want or never got, too tire to work, and too tired to make love to your mate—that's right, I said it! I don't mean have sex; I mean make love. That takes time, effort, and energy, energy that you give to others but not to your mate. The primary excuse is the kids. The primary thief is your job. It doesn't take up your time; you give it your time.

Chasing that almighty buck in the name of comfort does not happen without costing you something in other areas of your life. Though statistics vary, the divorce rate is allegded to be over 50 percent now and even higher in the black community, upwards around 60 to 73 percent, especially when you count second and third marriages (ref: divorcesource.com; divorcesaloon.com). That usually consists of a blended family and assorted ex-wives and ex-husbands (otherwise known as baby daddies and baby mamas) to deal with. The experts will tell you that most divorces are because of money. I think money is an alibi to the truth. If many of you break it on down, you'll find that the only thing you haven't paid is attention to one another like you used to when you were trying to snag one another, and once you got snagged, you went downhill physically and failed to give one another the physical attention you needed, and you blamed that on lack of money to supplement your not being physical—no vacations, falling behind the Jones, spending more money on a car per month than on each other—when you know darn well that the best things in life are free!

And please spare me with that "it's what's inside that counts" crap. Negro, please! That's an excuse for being too lazy to exercise and sacrifice a dozen shrimp and a slab of barbecue ribs. Black-on-black crime is black folk cooking and serving up food—soul food—that is killing us. Barbecue, chitterlings, smothered anything with a side of mashed potatoes with gravy, a full, fat belly, burp, and a smile is why you don't feel like emptying the trash or cuddling (Yuk!) with your wife, but you've got to make those sacrifices.

We must respect our bodies and what it houses—our heart, liver, kidneys, ligaments, blood flow … Filling our bodies with beer, cigarette smoke, dope (pick your own poison), and soul food is dumb! Now I realize that you don't have to cut out *all* foods. Try fewer times or in smaller portions. That, along with regular checkups with your doctor—another thing we fail to do, especially men at forty years and beyond—and even minimal exercise could mean the difference between a marriage and a divorce, a traditional family and a fatherless family, being weak and doubtful or having enough energy to go that extra mile. To many people it'll not take much of a change. To others, it's a lifestyle change. To those who love and depend on you, it's appreciated.

Now, I realize what I am about to say is going to ruffle some feathers, but the church has its share of responsibility in this matter of personal health as well. God is certainly our nucleus, but the church (and other religious places of worship) is our largest institution with a captive audience in the world, guided by selected individuals with more influence than many probably deserve. We are a society of followers, and while the church's place is to teach God's word, part of its responsibility should be to insist that its congregation has access to healthy foods. Oh, by the way, let's start with the pastor. Build accessible grocery stores in poor neighborhoods and lower the prices of its healthy foods and leave off a wing of the new sanctuary. Consistently teach healthy eating habits and insist on exercise and healthy living like you do on tithing. It does not take much strength to lift a dollar bill or a check to put in the church plate, so a consistent effort to talk to its people about ways to deal with obesity (and finances) goes by the wayside. Poverty, obesity, and the church should go hand in hand. In the poorest parts of our world, when people are hungry and malnourished, they are but skin and bones. Again, I say only in America can you be poor and obese.

And lest I forget, let's value one another more. Let's stop killing one another. Stop believing that black people are worthless. Stop thinking that any black person dead doesn't matter to anyone. It matters. It matters to the mother of that boy, girl, man, or woman. It matters to the wife of that man or to the husband of that woman. It matters to grandmothers who raised their children and who are now raising their children's children. It matters to cousins and uncles and aunts. It also matters to God. If you have a shred of sensitivity in you, stop the madness. Stop ripping apart our self-esteem and unity by calling one another nigger. Stop killing your own people! I heard a statement made once that basically said that the only way that one could be great to oneself is not what is done to your body – the clothes you wear or great physical attributes - but what you do to your mind.

Our thoughts do affect our reality. Perhaps it is as Stanley Crouch and Playthell Benjamin say in their thoughts, as recorded in the book *Reconsidering the Souls of Black Folk*, that tribalism is the father of racism. Slavery was in full swing in Africa well before

Negroes were kidnapped by or sold to white Americans. At that time, it was not thought of as slavery in the sense we know it to be now. But if it looks, walks, and quacks like a duck … It was based on the simple theory of supply and demand. In the above-mentioned book, the authors say that perhaps Negroes in Africa had already been crushed before meeting civilization. We have never overcome that. White folks didn't invent slavery; they just enhanced it, providing for themselves an advantage.

We must stop this two-piece and a pepper living where we just settle instead of expecting more of ourselves and our children, thinking that the little goals we accomplish are evidence of success. As long as we can get our two-piece and a pepper, we think we have made it. Our God is bigger than that. We must come to grips with the fact that we as a people, as a country, as God's people, are inextricably linked. Our success or failure is tied to one another. To hurt one of us is to hurt all of us. That is what we should be angry about.

Mentally

By that I mean get an education. We can't save the world by rapping about it, running a hundred yards is not enough, and dribbling is just that, dribble. While everything has its place in life, special opportunities are rare. General opportunities are everywhere. Being a multimillion-dollar sports star with no education beyond high school or a few years of handheld college courses is as risky as a baby with a loaded gun. There is nothing inherently wrong with money. It's like drinking and driving. When you mix money and no education, it's a deadly combination. Don't put all of your eggs in that one basket. Making money is not as hard as keeping it. But life is not about money. It's about family, friends, and taking full advantage of each day that God allows you. And make no mistake about it; you do not control your life. It can be taken away from you as quickly as you can bat your eye. And if it's not taken away, the quality of life can drift away slowly but surely. Specifically, your mind. Your mind is the most powerful weapon you have, and our "blackground" is evidence to the fact that we can overcome just about anything, except ourselves.

We as a people have accomplished so much. Much of it has been covered up by somebody else's story, otherwise known as history. We know about everyone else's story but our own, and when we try to learn about us or talk about us, some of the more "edumacated" black folk will try to stop us before we embarrass them in front of good, old white folks. And there are many good white folks out there. A lot if not most of them. But that still makes us black. There is no doubt in my mind that plenty is owed to black folks in general and American Negroes in particular. After thousands of Africans were shipped here, and thousands died on the way, the rest built this country as free slave labor so that the roots of good, honest white folk could be planted so deep as to still have a firm grip on this country while they ask why we black folk are always so angry or always asking for something free. We are indeed owed something. But the only thing asked for is a fair and equal shot at life, liberty, and pursuit of happiness, as is written in a constitution put together when black folk were barely considered much more than a piece of furniture, let alone included in it. However, seeing how easily we catch on and how we still have that work ethic and ability to survive on less and do more, I can see why the hesitancy is there to crack the door on equality. There is always that inner fear that we would not just keep up but surpass and take over—and then payback! I don't think so. Black folk just want a fair day's pay for a fair day's work along with equal perks and go on about our business. No revenge. No payback. Just a fair opportunity to succeed. That takes an education.

Call it a white man's education, a black man's education, go to an all-white school or a historically black school, I don't care—just get an education. Graduate. You'll figure out the rest later. Exercise your mind. Forget about payback and who owes you what. Leave white folk alone! We don't need that distraction. They're not killing more of us than we are. They're not trashing our neighborhoods; we are. They're not controlling the lung functions that cause us to inhale deeply to snort the cocaine or smoke the crack; we are. They're not pulling the trigger or dropping out of school at record pace; we are. They're not stopping at the stop sign and dropping the dirty pampers on the ground; we are. They're not throwing the empty forty-ounce bottles out of the window, trashing the areas where we live; we are. They're not hanging the car engines in the tree or dragging old cars in the backyard; we are. They're not forcing us to drive down the street with our kid(s) in the car, windows rolled up while we force cigarette smoke into their young, pink lungs, failing to buckle them up and claiming that we love them. We are. They're not forcing our young fourteen- and fifteen-year-old girls to open their legs to eighteen-, twenty-one-year-old and older boys, getting pregnant and dumping the kid(s) on their mothers; we are. It is not the responsibly of white folk to teach our young boys not to have sex until they are in a committed marriage because the parents don't believe in that, respect black girls as the mothers of our future, or teach black men how to love a black woman. That is up to us.

And just why is it that allegedly over 70 percent of black babies are born out of wedlock? Does being broke, jobless, hopeless, or uneducated make you horny? Leave white folk alone! Focus on the good of all people. Yes, we all can get along! So stop asking and start trying. Easier said than done, but in order for progress to show up, we must all give up something.

Economically

As I stated earlier, there is nothing inherently wrong with money. It's not how much money you have but how you use, save, or invest money. As a bonus, an education will show you how to use OPM, other people's money. To get right down to it, what we need is ownership. Stop being satisfied with paying on something and be more satisfied with paying off something. The first thing you do is take care of what you've got. Pay for what you have. Hold back on getting that new car and have the discipline to take that money you were so willing to sacrifice your child's education for and put it toward paying for or paying off your house early. If you don't have a house, get one—small, single family home, large two-story home, just as long as it's well within your "we can no longer go to the movies" budget. It is simply a dumb move to clamp a chain onto your ankle with the other end securely fastened to your house!

When that's paid for, get other people to pay you. Get rental property or start that business you have so passionately wanted. "I don't know what business I could go in," you whine with your finger up your nose. Well, while going into business doesn't always mean opening up a storefront and hiring employees—it's not meant for everyone—there are certainly too many black folk doing things that many people only wished they could do or do better. Utilize those skills everyone compliments you on to bring in some money for you and your family or your dreams. If you are tired of that glass ceiling, then create your own ceiling. Don't get greedy; get smart, but get something. Set yourself a budget. Someone else's, not your own made-up budget. Try Larry Burkett's budget, Dave Ramsey, or Crown Financial to name a few—in bookstores everywhere.

One of the best things we can do in the life of American Negroes everywhere is read more! I've never heard of a book being booked for injury to a child or an adult. Why don't we read? Many black males don't even know that there are many other parts of the newspaper other than the sports section! Hello! Keep up with world events, for heaven sakes! You don't have to become an expert at it, but at least know where Africa is on the map! Learn about Dow Jones and how to read a stock portfolio. Then maybe you can get one! This may be quite a shock to you, but most folk who are wealthy did not, I repeat *did not* get it from the lottery! That's a throw-your-money-away deal. If you just can't do what you want, do the best you can with what you have. That's going to take some patience. Hold back on getting some things you want today in order to secure your tomorrow, but still live for and enjoy today because, let's face it, right now that's all you've got, and it's only God's will that you'll see the end of this day. The greatest power—and the only thing that some folks will understand—is our economic power. One of, if not the most talked about subjects in the Bible is money and its influence on people. As an American Negro, we are going to have to speak with our economic power instead of our mouths. A lot of money goes through our hands because someone else wants it. Let's use it to our advantage. Everyone else does! Know the value of what you have and don't sell it or yourself short. Then let's pass on as much as we can to our families. Our future generations should not have to struggle as we did to gain their future.

There Goes the Hood:
Taking the Motor Out of the Tree

A few years ago, there was a debate in Dallas, Texas—and I'm sure this debate has, is, and will go on in other cities and states in America—about bringing in and building Section Eight housing in an affluent but predominantly white neighborhood in the northern part of the city. As most know, Section Eight is a low-income housing program instituted by the city allowing a blended mixture of classes throughout the city. These homes were to be built to blend in with its new community without disturbing its character. The only problem was the stereotypical idea of *there goes the neighborhood* mentality, along with the thoughts of it lowering home values and deteriorating the communities that most people move into to get away from the deteriorating communities they used to live in. There was much protest, as you can imagine, but the most interesting thing I observed was the reaction from black people who were not a part of this move yet basically understood why the mostly white community objected to this. The most interesting line I heard was from a black man who sounded as though he too was fed up with how black neighborhoods lacked self-pride and ownership. He said, "I don't blame white folk up there for not wanting black people to move into their neighborhood! You can't even get black folk to take the motor out of the tree!" Now I cleaned a little of that quote up a bit, but most blacks can clearly understand his line about taking the motor out of the tree. Most whites may not, but that one statement says it all.

For those who may not understand that statement, it refers to the fact that black men usually will use their yards to work on just about anything but mostly their old cars, and when working on an engine, they may have to pull the old engine out of the car. But to do that, instead of getting an engine hoist, they will rig a chain and pulley in the nearest tree in the yard that will hold it and hoist the engine out of the car to work on it whenever they can. That engine may stay in that tree for days, weeks, months, and even years whether it's in the front yard or back. The attitude is that as long as it is in their yard and they pay the rent or note, they can do whatever they want to do. How's that for improving the looks of a neighborhood? The meaning of the statement above was that black folk would carry that same mentality to other communities. The fact that it was a black man making this statement is proof that this is not acceptable to all black people nor is it exclusively an act that only black men do. But the real question seems to be who is following whom? When whites lived in certain neighborhoods and blacks moved in, there became a *white flight* to the suburbs when a predominant number of blacks moved into their neighborhood. Now, most of those predominantly white neighborhoods are predominantly black. However, blacks now want to move out of these neighborhoods to go to the suburbs, seemingly to get away from the "motor in the tree" blacks moving to where the whites before them moved to. What statement does that make?

What is happening to our predominately black lower- to middle-class communities has become embarrassing. Amongst ourselves we allow our home to deteriorate, although some may be of legitimate cause, perhaps due to a loss of job or illness or old age. However, there are too many without excuses. There seems to be a diminishing pride in our communities, and there is this pervasive attitude of *this is my property, and I'll do with it what I please, and if you don't like it, then that's your problem,* regardless of how your property reflects on the rest of the community, street, or neighborhood. This also causes a surge in HOAs (home owner associations). This is not a reflection on our neighborhoods as much as it is a reflection on our feelings toward one another. That lack of respect does not come from outside of the house but from the inside. As stated above, this is due to a pervasive attitude—attitude being the adamant word here because there are black communities with attitudes just the opposite. Wonderful, clean, and beautiful communities whether there are older communities or newer homes. Their expectations are different. Their attitude is different. Likeminded people seem to be drawn to one another or seek one another out, regardless of their race many times. My concern is that the norm seems to be otherwise. Has our reputation preceded us, and how difficult is it to change that reputation?

The Bigger Agenda

One thing that black people use as a driving force is the word pride. That is a scary word. Pride has been the cause of many downfalls from world wars to divorces. Pride is not for us to be. Pride is for others to be for us. And that's not free.

One of the most important things that we must do is stand back, step outside of ourselves, outside of our homes, our neighborhoods, our cities, our state, our country, and be reminded that there is a place and an agenda bigger than our own. Bigger than the black agenda. Bigger than the American Negroes agenda. Bigger than the African American or African agenda, and that is the agenda of the state of our world. Could it be that we are simply pawns in a larger plan? Could it be that while we are fighting amongst ourselves and diverting our attention to what white folks have done and are doing to us that there are others outside of our country planning to take over or destroy America? How we got here suddenly makes no difference. America is a superpower. That means there are those who would like nothing better than to knock us off. Not us as blacks or whites or Hispanics, etc. but us as Americans.

Stop for a minute and think about the world outside of our own. What really happened during the Cuban missile crisis? Would those missiles have only hit white people? How about Libya? How about Iran? What about all of the other countries that really don't like America? ISIS? Libya doesn't see color. Iran doesn't see color. Russia doesn't see color. They see the United States. And when it comes to the point where our country is threatened, we're not going to be worried about what white folk think of black folk or black-on-black crime. These people see no color. They see a country. And they would like nothing better than to be the ones to put the notch in their guns to say that they are the ones who have destroyed our country and our freedoms. It's times like this that we must settle our differences and come together as a country and realize that we cannot make it without the full force of America. All of America. They are all, however, probably very pleased with the infighting and diversions we bring on ourselves while they send in or pay off spies who give out our technological secrets and strategic plans. They hear and know about the animosities between the races in this superpower we've put together. They laugh at the vicious attacks our politicians throw at each other. They love the divide between the Democrats and Republicans, Protestants and Catholics, Muslims and Christians, blacks and whites. United we stand, divided we fall.

Our inability to put aside bickering and live with our differences puts us all in a very threatened position around the world. We must get it together not for ourselves as blacks or American Negroes but for the sake of America. Black people have fought and died for this country regardless of how we got here. There is a bigger agenda out there whose intent is to destroy us all while our backs are turned, fighting one another within.

We as a black people need to be more world conscious. Follow what's going on outside of our own problems. Yes, we still need to be accepted as equal partners in this land of liberty and justice, the free and the brave. We must never give up that fight. And perhaps we shouldn't see that as a fight but as a claim on opportunity. But somebody's gotta be watching the backdoor. We as American Negroes have a responsibility to defend and protect this country as well. There is no sacred oath preventing us from turning off black sitcoms and turning our televisions, radios, and newspapers to political issues. Not to be experts but to at least have a familiar understanding of what's going on outside of our borders. Stop looking at political and world issues as boring. Broaden your intellect and perspective on issues that concern not just American Negroes but Americans. Become a part of a larger and bigger picture. A bigger solution. Here's an agenda. Blacks are approximately 14 percent of America's population. Blacks are allegedly 46 percent of America's HIV infections. Black women were allegedly 64 percent of all HIV infections between 2008 -2011 (avert.org). Causes vary, but two are: infected black prisoners released back into the population and the dreaded *down low*. Fight over that for a while.

Remember Rwanda!

The World

Allow me to just touch on one other point of concern that seems to be a bit taboo. It is being said, and actions seems to validate the claim, that black women are being strategically placed in positions of authority in the professional world in order to be pitted against and to block the promotions, power, and authority of black men by whites who are in control. That it is easier to control or push forward a black woman than it is to control or pull back a black man. This is not only an advantage to the whites in control at keeping black men at bay from higher level positions but easier to not only make a black woman work twice as hard, but to be more willing to put down, demoralize, or show cause to demote another black man—or woman for that matter. It makes a demotion or lack of promotion look like a race issue instead of an EEO claim situation. Many women already have a *liberative* attitude that is becoming more and more pervasive in our society and creeping even more so in the black culture. This is a serious issue that can and in many ways has already created a division between black men and black women, not to mention divisiveness among black women in the workplace.

There is room at the top for both. We do not need for there to be an either/or issue. We must use our heads to think and our eyes to see beyond the here and now and see a much broader picture. We are too smart to be used that way. We must always be fair across the board and not let our personal feeling get in the way of our professional responsibilities. This is not the first time in history that blacks have had opportunities as professionals. We have run entire cities, banks, businesses, fire departments, police department, and city services in various parts of this country since as far back as anyone can remember—our own cities. It is nothing new. Being pitted against one another is nothing new either. Stop the madness! We cannot make it apart. We must work together. Preserve our unity for one another but fairness to all. Let's preserve our dignity.

The Bible that we hold so near and dear has prophecies that have proven themselves true for years. Jesus was a Jew in human form. And He chose the Jews to be His chosen people though later included the Gentiles of the world. Even *He* fought for and was intimately involved in the welfare and well-being of His people. His fight was ultimately for the good of all people. Why is it that when we as a black people talk about the welfare and well-being of our people—not as a chosen people, not with the intent of dominance—we are accused of being segregationists, bitter, or antiwhite? What we do should be for the good of all. Let us not be deceived as to who the true enemy is. I earlier talked about faith. The problem with always talking about faith and God is that it starts to feel so good that we let Satan tip right past us on his way to making our lives very challenging. You cannot believe in God who protects us without asking the question "Who is He protecting us from?" God's voice is soft and comforting, but His actions are loud and commanding, so we very often miss His voice because of all of the noise around us. Folks, there is an enemy that wants to make us think that our problems are physical or racial or within. That our problem is one another. Satan is out to destroy, but he can't do it himself. He must make us destroy ourselves, and he is doing a great job in the black communities. He is the elephant. You cannot afford to ignore him or allow him to influence your thinking. Turn around!

A New and Living Way

Let me end this with a quote from the one who *brung* us (excuse my English). The word of God. The Bible.

> Let us hold fast the confession of our hope without
> wavering, for He who promised is faithful; and let
> us consider how to stimulate one another to love
> and good deeds, not forsaking our own assembling
> together, as is the habit of some, but encouraging
> one another, and all the more, as you see the day
> drawing near. For if we go on sinning willfully
> after receiving the knowledge of the truth, there
> no longer remains a sacrifice for sins, but a certain
> terrifying expectation of judgment, and the fury of
> a fire which will consume the adversaries.
> —Hebrews 10:22–27 NAS

If we continue this cycle of losing hope and respect for one another without encouraging one another to our highest potential, inspiring one another to the greatness that has been proven by us, and stop hating ourselves as many do instead of coming together in unity, not only as a people but as a country, our actions will soon catch up with us, and there will no longer be a way out of the web we tangle ourselves in.

Why are we afraid to dream anymore? Big dreams. Your future starts with a dream. God is waiting on dreamers. He dares you to dream. He's waiting to take you there. Martin Luther King Jr. gave us that message as well when he said, "I have a dream!" Do you have a dream? I mean a dream so big only God can pull it off. Do you dare to dream that dream? Is fear holding you back? I talk about the children of Israel a lot because we so identify with them. I heard a preacher say something once that really opened my mind. He said that God did not rescue the children of Israel from Egypt to get them out of something, but to take them somewhere. They complained all of the way, not understanding that, and many died never having fulfilled their life's journey. We as a black people have been rescued from slavery not to get us out of something but to take us somewhere. Our dreams were deferred by our freedom. Many have died never having fulfilled their life's journey. Afraid to step out on the faith we claim to have. Afraid to fail. Not succeeding is not failure. Failure is never having tried to succeed.

> "There's nothing more dangerous than sincere ignorance and conscientious stupidity."
> —Martin Luther King Jr.

Sincere ignorance is to walk purposely and boldly down a blind path. To defend your lack of knowledge for the sake of black pride or stubborn defiance. Or the act of honestly doing something for a long period of time the wrong way because no one told you the right way. Lack of knowledge because the truth was hidden from you, oftentimes on purpose. Like being told that smoking is harmless and not having access to the truth.

Conscientious stupidity is to be aware of your lack of knowledge or ignorance and doing nothing to correct it. Doing something that is obviously wrong on purpose because it fits your way of thinking and refusing to do the right thing.

My People, Who Are Called by My Name

I was born in a place that hid its bad character well; at least from me it did. Though too young to really understand but too old to ignore it, deep down I knew. I didn't say anything though. Sometimes you learn a lot by just listening and watching. Sometimes I didn't even know I was listening or that I was even watching, but my eyes always seemed to catch what I didn't see, and my ears heard what I didn't hear. It just put it up there somewhere in my head for when I'd need it, I guess. It always came out of nowhere. The words, that is. The sights and sounds of life.

Somehow I knew right from wrong. I guess all of those whippings I got made me just know, or scared to death not to. And those hellfire, damnation sermons my momma made us go and hear at the church sounded like home, only not as loud. But Momma always seemed to be running scared. Mostly on the inside, but sometimes a little of that would come out. Momma used to talk to us—me and my sisters and brothers—in what I called the Z frame. That was my own way of trying to keep up with things I didn't understand. I would put it in sort of a riddle that usually only I could solve, but that way it stayed in my head. Z frame was Momma's way of skipping A through Y and going straight to Z, straight to the point. Usually because she didn't have time to explain but mostly because she knew we wouldn't understand and always because she was just too mad to talk about it calmly. She wasn't mad all of the time, and most of the time her being mad was not at us but at something deep inside of her that protected us. We had some fun times too. When she laughed, it was like the school bell ringing for time to go home just after a hard test. She was there for everybody, but everybody wasn't there for her. But she just kept on doing what she could. She had big dreams too. You could just tell, but she never got the chance to follow through on any of them. So she put all of her energy into raising us.

There were six of us. Split right down the middle—three boys and three girls. I guess you could say I was the odd one. I always felt like I was born at the wrong place at the wrong time, like I should have been born in the olden days. Perhaps I showed it from time to time. I didn't have a lot of friends, but I had enough to have some fun.

Daddy was sort of the referee. Daddy was a big man but soft-spoken in a loud sort of way. He didn't have to say much. You just sort of knew what he wanted. I admired him from a distance. Kinda like a movie star. But I didn't tell him that. I didn't want to bother him. He was a very hardworking man who loved his peace and quiet every once in a while. He was a gentle giant. He gave great hugs too. We were sort of like a lion and his cubs, only he didn't lick you, but you knew he would if that's what you needed. Maybe that was only how I wanted him to be.

I called him Daddy, and my mom was Momma. Sometimes I would go to the market with Momma or to the auto store with Daddy. There I would see different people. I never really paid attention to differences in the color of the people we saw, at first.

I knew that I was darker than white people, but it wasn't something I thought about a lot. But as I got older, it seemed I got more confused. Mostly about who I was or who we were. That seemed to change everywhere we went. Outside of the home was very different. There was very little love there. We, people like me, dressed a little differently, talked differently, and our hair was different too. I supposed that was why we were called so many different names. Some made my daddy very angry inside. Some made him a little upset, and some he seemed to accept. I was taking all of this in, but I didn't quite understand it all. Maybe that's why Momma talked her Z talk. She didn't want us to not know or to forget any of our experiences. She shielded us from a lot, which meant that she took the blows in our stead and sort of told us how it hurt. She didn't know that it hurt me anyway. I could feel her pain, but I didn't tell her that.

We grew up fast in those days. You had to or you'd die slowly without knowing what hit you. But death for us was different. You first died on the inside. The outside was just there to keep us from bumping into one another. Whatever or whoever we were, there seemed to be a lot of us in that one body. The thing that disturbed Daddy and Momma the most was the names. It was like an evolution. We have many names with many meanings. Now that I'm older and wiser, all of those things I heard and saw back then are starting to pay off.

The things that made my mom talk to us the way she did and made my dad so angry that he said nothing were puzzling to me. Some say the stronger you are the braver you are. But that's not the way I saw it. It seems to be that the weaker you are the tougher you act. It's all a game. No respect, and that lack of respect earns you a different name. Your name determines your status, and it also gives an evolutionary picture of the history—more like *his* story—of the man of color. Sticks and stones may break my bones, but words will never hurt me? I'd rather get hit with sticks and stones. With that, at least the pain would eventually go away. Sticks and stones only hurt on the outside. It's the inside that stays with you. It changes you.

The first word was nigger. It hurts me to even say this word, but believe it or not, this word outranked *boy*. This word was a double-edged sword. It identified or branded you physically and demeaned and humiliated you psychologically. That was back then. It still feels the same today, primarily to those who know our history. This word seemingly came from the early biblical times as a symbolic representation of people from North Africa. It is also pulled from the name of a river in West Africa flowing through Nigeria. This was Niger (ni'jer). Nigger is its dirty, no good for nothin' version. Now, if you were approached by an educated ignoramus, you could graduate to a more dignified version of this word, "niggra." This word is from those who are intellectually astute—or *asstupid*. You know, the ones who have figured out that little-known secret of our ancestral, nomadic tribe called the Negroids. Cute. But before you laugh, check your nearest dictionary. It's there! It must have been added in by one of those asstupid intellectuals. Well, Webster also defines Negro as "any person with some Negro ancestors." And if Webster said it, it must be true, right? That must be that Negroid race referred to earlier. Excuse me, but did not man originate in the land of the Negroids? Wow! I guess that makes us all Negroes then. That also means that the whole world is going through an acute case of black-on-black crime!

There's gotta be a way out of this. A way to separate us. Hey! How about calling us *colored*? Even a Negro knows the differences in colors, even if we don't know who all are under this umbrella called Negro, having ancestors and all. Okay, then let's use the color black. Besides, it allows us to have a respectable counterpart. That's only fair. It's either that or *boy*! Now there's a word symbolic of everything you don't want to be called. At least it recognizes you as a human being. This used to be a good word. It's what our fathers used to call us. It had love and pride in it. Now you don't even call a boy a boy without a fight.

But let's correct this Negroid business. We—nigger, niggra, Negroid, Negro, colored, black, or boy—are all descendants from Africa, known as the cradle of civilization, and our most distinguishing features is not our differences in color but our afro! A little puff of kinky hair that says, "I am love, I am Negro, I am Afro American." Makes you feel real patriotic, doesn't it? Now breaking this down, an Afro American is an American with an afro. If you agree with that, then you'll also have to agree with the fact that there is a whole other race of people walking amongst us with dark and multicolored skin but straight, processed, curly, faded, dreadlocked, braided, and bald heads. I guess that makes them straight Americans; processed Americans, curly Americans, dreadlock Americans, braided Americans, and last but not least—or none at all—our bald Americans. I'm sure they'll be pleased to finally get the recognition they so richly deserve. Alas, there is a country from which all human beings derived. The place where scholars, secular and theologians alike, agree on. Africa. Though James Baldwin called us American Negroes, I guess that makes us African Americans. Right back where we started from. And you know, it sort of feels like home. I think I'll stay for a while and raise some children. And who knows, maybe, just maybe, when I'm all rested up a bit, I'll start a new race!

Information

While researching and gathering information, I stumbled on an article entitled, "Black Power of the Purse, A Consumers' Republic: The Politics of Mass Consumption in Postwar America," by Lizabeth Cohen (Alfred A. Knopf, New York, January 2003). Also, I came across an article entitled "Black-on-Black Violence" done by Sistahspace.com.

I'd like to give you some interesting information written as a combination of both articles, noting the similarities in thought and conclusions.

If African American consumer activism reached a new height during the 1930s, it grew from deep roots. Several historical efforts to improve black circumstances through consumer action prepared the ground. The consumer boycott was the major strategy with which blacks had protested on a mass scale the imposition of Jim Crow laws in the South in the late nineteenth and early twentieth centuries, particularly those mandating the segregation of trolley cars in all major southern cities. Although the streetcar boycotts failed, the fact that the determination of thousands of black riders had managed to deprive urban transit companies of profit for periods ranging from a few weeks to a couple years, and even to drive a few into bankruptcy, remained an important memory of resistance passed on from generation to generation. When black leaders in Lynchburg, Virginia, condemned a new segregation law relegating blacks to the back of trolley cars as "a gratuitous insult … to everyone with a drop of Negro blood," and urged a boycott to "touch to the quick the white man's pocket. *'Tis* there his conscience lies," they helped create a model for retaliating against discrimination in the purchase of goods and services through withdrawing consumer patronage. … Most significantly, by mobilizing as consumers, African Americans participated in a broader political culture of dissent where "*the consumer*" became viewed as a legitimate and effective agent of protest, particularly for women and blacks who were marginalized from the mainstream of politics and the labor movement. In contrast to electoral and producer power, the strength of consumer power lay not so much with permanent organizations as with the potential from mobilizing mass action by individual consumers. Although depression-era blacks did not link the economic rights of the consumer to the political rights of the citizen nearly as much as women consumer activists did or as they would a few years later in the context of World War II, the seeds were planted: a slogan in the Chicago buying campaign was "Use your buying power as you use your ballot," … (Cohen;Knof)

By the 1930s, both W.E.B. Du Bois and E. Franklin Frazier acknowledged that wherever statistics were recorded, black males were killing one another with withering frequency, at rates far exceeding those of whites. (One should keep in mind that comparisons between black and white homicide rates in the nineteenth century are misleading because white homicide rates did not take into account the thousands of southern blacks who were lynched and murdered with impunity by whites. Less than 1 percent of those responsible were ever arrested and convicted.) Nowhere was the carnage more evident than in the swelling ghettos of U.S. cities. Evidence from a wide variety of sources consistently reveals that already high levels of violence within the black community rose sharply in the early twentieth century, especially in the urban areas.

The roots of black-on-black violence can be traced back to the previous century, the southern experience, and the system of criminal justice that took the place of slavery as a means of social control after emancipation. Long before the urban transformation of the black population that began with the Great Migration North in the second decade of this century, southern blacks were assaulting and killing one another at remarkable levels. By this time, blacks were also well aware that few whites cared whether they lived or died. The paradox of emancipation is that freedom removed the monetary value of blacks as white property, meaning that so long as their victims were also black and about who was murdered, raped, or robbed, or by whom. The seriousness of black-on-black crime was almost solely determined by the criterion of color. Trial transcripts reveal that "Whose nigger are you?" or "Whose nigger was he?" were common questions asked by magistrates at murder trials. ... In the world created by slaveholders, women were property--virtually the only, and probably the most satisfying, possession available to a male slave. The pattern continued after emancipation. Even in northern cities of the early twentieth century, an uneducated black male could readily possess and control. Like the wives of African chieftains, the number of females a man controlled provided evidence for all to see of his personal worth. The status to be gained from possessing a woman that other men wanted probably sharpened the competition as much as sexual gratification. Indeed, for too many young black males of black males of this period, manhood itself, as well as respect, depended on the number of women one could claim. In a real sense, homicide rates still provide a measure of the intensity of such sexual competition ... (Sistahspace)

The reason for including this was not to put you through information overload on a subject that you are probably tired of hearing about but to show how—though much has changed—we are still dragging many of those old habits and thoughts with us to the present times and handing off this slave mentality to our children. Years ago when our forefathers were in slavery in this country, those who were brave and relentless enough attempted to escape, and when they did, they headed for the woods. When Kunta Kinte escaped from slavery, he headed for the woods. When Harriet Tubman led our people by way of the Underground Railroad, she went by way of the woods. What I'm trying to say is that while we have been freed from slavery, we are still in the woods. Get out of the woods and go to where true freedom is. It's about understanding the big picture. There is always a big picture.

No Excuses Now?

(I'm just sayin'.)

On November 4, 2008, a new day dawned in America. Barack Hussein Obama became what many refer to as our first black president of these United States of America. A black man lifted to a place of being the man who runs the most powerful country in the world. Humpty Dumpty fell off the wall, and he was handed a broken country and asked to put it back together again. He has at his disposal all the king's horses and all the king's men, most of whom were loyal to another before him, but history in that regard is not so different from the other kings. Much has been said and written and talked about it. It still amazes me that with a population percentage of, what, 13 percent, 14 percent black/minority, a black man was elected president of white America. If every minority man, woman, and child in this country voted, we still would not have had enough votes—especially taking out those who couldn't or simply wouldn't vote—to elect a black man into the highest office in the land. Sounds a little suspect to me, or am I just not giving America, or President Barak Obama for that matter, credit for its intelligence? Now don't get it twisted. I'm just saying! Perhaps you're not giving me credit for *my* intelligence, huh?

The thing that interested me the most out of all of this (Or should I say *things*. You know a brother can't stop at one thing.) were some of the reactions of black people after the election. Particularly the continued statement of "We now have no excuse!" I, and I'm sure many others, took that to mean that now that we have a black man as president of the United States of America, we as a black people—a minority people—can no longer use the excuse that we are not capable of greatness. We can no longer hold ourselves back with the excuse that we are not good enough. We can no longer say the words "I can't" because President Barack Obama has now shown us that we can. Does this mean that before President Obama was elected we saw ourselves as not capable of achieving greatness? Have we forgotten our past? A better question is do we know our past, or even better, have we passed our past on or done as the educated intellectuals suggest, leave the past in the past. *Forgetaboutit?* Is this what we thought of ourselves pre-Obama? And do we really think that this will open the door to honesty, fairness, our slice of the American pie, a balanced playing field? Did it do that for Colin Powell or Adam Clayton Powell? Were we not encouraged by Shirley Chisholm? Were we not inspired by Lewis Howard Latimer or Frederick M. Jones? Did we not move ahead with Mordecai Johnson or Dr. Charles Drew? Were we not pushed by Mary McLeod Bethune? I could go on and on and on. So, with all due respect, what makes President Barak Obama, a man standing on the shoulders of these people, more inspirational than them? Or more influential than what your son or daughter will be? I'm not taking away President Obama's achievements and hard work; I'm saying that if others didn't inspire us, what will make him any different? We must stop riding the waves of other people and start riding our own wave. We have no excuses *now?* Really? Where have we been since our freedom?

Another thing that has moved me is this whole thing about being a Democrat, Republican, or an Independent. The Democratic part concerns me the most. If my research of history and books serves me correctly, black folk were the Republicans before we "followed the leader" to the Democratic Party. Now don't get it twisted. We have the privilege of being able to vote any party we choose—and unfortunately we have the freedom to not vote, which totally throws me after all that we have gone through to get the right to vote, but that's another book. The problem is that we vote for parties and not people. We vote color or status and not views and intentions. Black people are traditionally a conservative people, and I welcome you to challenge me on this. Most of the things that the Democratic Party stands for looks like, sounds like, smells like a liberal. What's up with that? Most blacks are pro-life. The Democratic Party is majority pro-choice. Most blacks believe that marriage and all of its rights should be between a man and a woman. The Democratic Party is very liberal on that as well. Most blacks are very conservative on gay rights issues. The Democratic Party is very liberal on that as well. I could go on and on about that. So what's up with that? I'm just saying. Are we changing? Oh by the way, the Republican Party is pro-life, believes that marriage should be between a man and a woman, and is very conservative on the gay rights issue. I'm just saying. In the words of Marvin Gaye, "What's going on?" Oh yeah, what would Jesus do? He would want you to vote for the man that supports His agenda (the most if necessary), regardless of the party. Jesus rides on neither donkeys nor elephants. It ain't that kind of party to Him.

I'm just sayin'.

Concluding Notes

There's an elephant in the room.

Stop walking around it as if it isn't there!

Face the elephant, even if it looks like us, and you face your fears and will see your own problems.

Stop standing with your back to the mirror. Turn around, and the elephant will disappear.

Stop wasting time blaming others!

Grow your own trees. Hold on to your roots.

Nothing is simple. Nothing is easy.

Remember what Jesus did for you.

Let's stop consuming one another!

The Ultimate Solution:
If It Were Mine …

We must take ownership of our daily walk in life. It is the only way to stop the downward slide.

When I walk into a restaurant, I must consider it as my business and treat it that way. If I leave paper on the floor or chairs out, I have to ask myself what I would do if this was my business.

If I walked into a grocery store, picked up an item on one side of the store and decided I no longer wanted it, if this was my store, would I simply leave the package of chicken on a shelf in the canned goods isle? If it were my hotel or motel, would I trash it? If it was my blood brother, would I shoot him in an argument? My sister, would I slap, hit, or abuse her regardless of what was done? Would I kidnap and rape my own sister or mother? Would I serve my child food I would not eat, or prepare it in an un-sanitized environment or drop it on the floor, pick it up, and serve it to them? Would I do or say the things I do or say to people I love and care deeply about?

If I took ownership of every person I ran into, every store visited or owned, or every word I said to people, I would then be forced to treat them the way I would want to be treated if it were me. I would then be forced to change. Change the way I looked at my people. Change the way I looked at all people. If I took ownership of everyone, everything, and my every word, I would have to change. Because how I live matters. Not to only me, but to everyone I come in contact with. It's about R-E-S-P-E-C-T.

A Thought

When you go to the grocery store and buy food, do you usually take a bag of groceries and stick it in the back window of your car—each car—and simply leave it there in cases of emergencies? Or take a loaf of bread you bought and stick in your glove compartment? Then take a bag and put one on the dining room table or maybe put a bag of rice in your room in the drawer? How about tucking a frozen dinner in your purse or a hoagie in your briefcase? Sounds a bit silly, doesn't it? Why would you do that? The need for food is driven by something within you that says you have depleted the energy that your body needs. The purpose of the food is for consumption, and the purpose for consumption is for restoration and strength. But in this process, you didn't have to first go and learn all over again how to eat. You know that already.

One day, while burdened down, my spirit was drained and heavy, and my first reaction (which is a blessing in and of itself) was to run to my Bible. A good source of nutrition whose purpose is for restoration and strength. But I realized that I did not have to learn how to read the Bible all over again. I had consumed enough of it to realize that what I needed to do was to use the sustenance I already had in me to make it through that particular crisis. I knew how to walk yet continued to rely on that crutch. The Word of God—the Bible—is tucked away in all areas of our lives for quick retrieval. Like food, God's word is made to be eaten, for the purpose of consumption, and the purpose of consumption is for restoration and strength. But in the process, you didn't have to first go and learn it all over again. The Bible is given to us not to be physically tucked away in every accessible corner of our lives but to be consumed— eaten—and used in times you may not be able to get to it physically. My emphasis is not to tell you to stop running to God's word but to convince you—and for some, raise the question—that you have enough knowledge of God's word within you (or should) to sustain you in a crisis. You do have enough, don't you? Nuff Said. I'm just sayin'.

My Visit to Africa

Home Sweet Home

God blessed me to be able to take my sixteen-year-old daughter to Africa during the writing of this book. It was in the month of our observance of what is referred to as black history month in Texas and other states that recognize and set aside this time to reflect on the accomplishments and struggles of the American Negro in the United States primarily, and abroad in general. We went on a mission trip to South Africa, Johannesburg area—"Joburg" as it is referred to. It was difficult to believe the history and the present life of our roots having been in such a beautiful land. With about 41 percent unemployment, the difference between the wealthy and the poor was like night and day. Like black and white. That is if you look at it in the measurement of money. But we had a chance to look at black African people from the inside out. We went to their neighborhoods, their homes. We walked their dirt and gravel roads, held their children, worked alongside them in their yards, planting gardens of cabbage and beets and beans and spinach. We watered their soil, used their bathrooms, were invited into their cramped, small but clean homes. We looked into one another's eyes and saw a reflection of one another but were separated by language for the most part. Yet we communicated with our hearts and touches and prayers and an occasional voluntary interpreter. But our histories communicated well. They were by all standards poor in treasures and tangible assets but rich in dreams, wants, and aspirations. Strong in struggle and champions in survival.

There was a strange peace in the middle of it all. The sound you hear just before the word "Charge!" Billy Graham put it best. He said that peace was that "glorious and wonderful time when all the world stands around, reloading." I will never forget the image of walking into, working in the yard of, and meeting a small-framed, older African lady who greeted us with joy and open arms, praising God as she spoke to us. The joy she had in the Lord was evident to be much deeper than her problems could reach. After accomplishing our mission there, as I walked out of her yard, I looked back to wave, and I couldn't help but notice, just to the right, on a small patch of grass, a rock dug into the ground and painted over with red paint, and the words written on it in white paint said Home Sweet Home. She smiled at me as if to say thank you. I pulled out my camera and snapped a picture of the rock. She called out to me in a surprised but joyful tone, and with a strong Zulu dialect of English, as best she could asked, "What are you doing?"

"Taking a picture there," I said.

"Of what?" she said.

"Of your rock that says Home Sweet Home," I joyfully said back. She burst out in a proud laugh and walked over to the rock.

"Get near and let me take a picture of you next to the rock!" I shouted.

"Okay!" she said joyously as she wiped her hands on the apron that hung from her waist, and she scurried over to the rock and laughed as I focused and snapped the picture. She then waved good-bye to me, and we both left each other better than we were before we met.

As I walked away down that dirt road to the next home, I thought to myself, *I will probably never see her again in my life.* That is why what you say to a person should make them better, because it could be the last memory of them you will ever have. My last memory of this lady was a smile and a wave good-bye. Then God reminded me of one very important thing that we both share. The same Father. I will indeed see her again. That made me smile. That made it easier to leave and move on to the next possibility, to the next memory.

That's what we are, possibilities. While in Africa, I noticed numerous similarities in their history and ours. Their past struggles with Apartheid, America's struggle with slavery. Africa was forced to give, and America was allowed to receive. Africa refused to accept their Union (their version of a constitution) and rebelled due to the fact that it was a document put together by white Africans without black consent, input, or knowledge, or risk being branded anti-African. American blacks were forced to accept a constitution also put together by white Americans, while not free and without consent, input, or knowledge, and were expected to follow it or else be branded anti-American.

Black Africans took to the streets to march in protest for unfair treatment and for inclusion, only to be met by troops ordered to stop them at all cost. That cost was innocent lives of young and old, unarmed black Africans, shot and beaten in their own streets for expressing their freedom of speech. Black Americans also took to the streets of America to march in protest of racism and for inclusion, only to be met by troops, water hoses, dogs, and military guns, beaten and shot down in the streets for freedom of expression.

Mandela jailed for twenty-seven years at that time. Martin Luther King killed forever.

I went through the Apartheid Museum. We were allowed to enter but only by way of how it was done in the past. We were given identity badges that gave us white or nonwhite status. After entering, we were to give our status cards to a guard and go before a committee of white men (now only a large wall picture of them sitting at a table) who gave us final determination on our status of being black, colored, or white and either allowed or denied entry. Inside there were pictures, slides, and movies of Africa's struggle. How they were forced to work in the minefields, many dying amongst those deep, dark rocks, with their bodies falling in the midst of a fortune of gold. Mostly young, strong black males who spent their entire lives in that hole, with only three candles for light, searching for what they could not have themselves, gold.

Going to Africa was like stepping back in time for me. The only advantage to that was knowing that they were only a step behind us, and victory was soon to come by the grace of God. Though victory was sure to come, there would be a lifelong struggle to protect freedom and rights. Things are no longer the way they used to be in Africa, but there is still a long way to go. The gap between the have and have-nots is so very obvious. The only thing they were given was their freedom. Then they were seemingly thrown out into a large field with small adobe dwellings and tin huts—shantytowns— now called home. Estimates suggest there were over 120,000 black Africans in the area we visited, where mostly grandmothers, their daughters, and their daughters' children lived.

Not very many men were living with these families. One particular area was called Diepsloot with its shantytown area. In spite of how it looked—after all, we were Americans used to having much—the poverty and HIV epidemic that consumed this place are not what I will remember from my visit. I will remember how wonderful and beautiful the people are there. How accepting of us they were with smiles on their faces and all of the wonderful little children. They were not all dressed in loincloths and carrying spears; they were normal, loving children who just wanted a hug and some attention. And some candy.

Most of my daughter's and my stay in Africa consisted of hard work. Backpack and shovel in hand, walking the streets of the poorest areas in Joburg/Pretoria. But we did get a chance to ride and look at the vastness and beauty of the land. The mountains and rolling hills. The openness just shouted, "Freedom!" We were able to go to a vast safari reserve where troops of lions lie in the road, rare wild dogs run in packs like hyenas, and huge vultures line the trees, waiting on a mistake to be made. Ostriches stick their long necks up in cautious anticipation as mountain goats balance themselves on the side of jagged hills, all in their natural habitat though separated by acres of fence that seem to stretch for miles. You felt a sense of helplessness and danger in a sort of Garden of Eden, being in their house, on their land, and in their space. We were invading their sanctuary, and some let us know that they did not like that. You had to respect them.

It only rained enough to keep things beautiful. Never long and never hard. God takes care of this land. While it was very evident that the people in this area were poor, it was also very evident that this land was rich. In the midst of poverty, rocks, and weeds, there were beautiful flowers and roses of all colors and of all kinds growing everywhere and in every yard. It was as if you could spit on this land, and what you last ate would grow there in a matter of days. The land was hungry to help these people. We felt good about the gardens we planted. The people wanted them and expected to eat of the bounty as soon as God ordered it to reveal itself from under the soil.

And let's not forget about the children. They were everywhere. To walk upon a small child on the dusty, dirt roads we walked was like finding a gold coin in the mud. All you had to do was wipe off the dirt and clean it up a bit to discover its beauty and value. Coming from America, I was surprised to see the young babies walking the roads without close, if any, supervision. We would panic in America, but this wasn't America. I thought to myself, *Who would want to kidnap them to add another mouth in the house to feed?* But this was the mythical village we always talk about. Here, it takes a village. People didn't take what wasn't theirs.

They knew how one another felt. They loved their children. One wonders why they continue to have children in such a desperate situation. I chose not to ask that question. They are human, just as I am. They have wants and needs and a life worth of love that must be emptied from them and given to someone. They too want to be loved and oftentimes get it from dishonest men with mixed feeling and little manhood to offer. Little of anything to offer. So they give themselves each other. Sometimes to a fault. Sometimes that's all you've got to give. That's no excuse nor is it condoned, but the children are now here. In our walks from home to home, we did not see very many homes with men in them. Mostly older women with younger women and their siblings. Perhaps the men were out working. Perhaps they just wandered in at night to relieve themselves with women who saw it as receiving attention and love. Perhaps in their minds this way everyone got what they wanted. Perhaps not.

HIV is one of many epidemics in Africa. There is a chance you take with every encounter. The soil that grows this epidemic is poverty and lack of education. No economic base for the people means no jobs, no health care, inadequate medical care, and all of that is enough to make you not care. If this doesn't sound familiar to you, allow me to refresh your memories. In America, the number-one killer amongst black people between the ages of twenty-five and forty-four at this time is HIV/AIDS, a statistic given by a speaker, Phil Wilson, the director of the Black AIDS Institute center, on this virus. On a radio show I was listening to, an article read in a locally published black newspaper in Dallas said that 120 prisoners are released from prisons every month with HIV, and they will usually have a sexual encounter within forty-eight hours of their release. According to the CDC and most any statistic found, it will state that more than half of all new HIV diagnoses reported in the United States in 2003 were black, and though the figures vary, black men now face a rate higher than whites and Latinos to be diagnosed with HIV. It is also stated that black women represented 72 percent of all new HIV/AIDS cases at that time. These numbers are for black Americans, not African Americans.

The biggest culprits to the spread of this disease are poverty, lack of primary health care and access to medicine, and the fact that most of these victims' primary health care is the emergency room. Racism is still the fuel that runs this engine. However, America is a land of access. We now have much more of an ability as American Negroes to access this information and to make wise choices. With this access to knowledge, poverty is becoming more of a scapegoat. You don't have to be rich to say no. You don't have to be wealthy to enter a public library to gain knowledge that affects you personally. You may have a challenge convincing others to give you a chance at a job, but that does not prevent you from making wise choices as it pertains to yourself and what you do or don't do. There is no cure for AIDS, but there is a cure for ignorance. One creates the other, and if you can figure out which one that is, you have shown that you are smart enough to avoid it, thus taking away your excuse. AIDS in the black community is another large elephant sitting in the room that we make believe isn't there. We walk around it, not through it. The choice is simple. Wake up now or never wake up again.

Africa is a mirror image of America in many ways. Blacks have always done better while in the midst of a struggle where we are unified for a common cause. But when we get what we want, we tend to relax to the point of a deep sleep, until we are suddenly woken up by more trouble. With AIDS, we seem to have gone into a coma. My question is this: if so many of us are dying of AIDS, why don't we hear about it every day? Most of us probably have friends, relatives, or associates with HIV. Why do we rarely hear of someone we know dying of AIDS? I would guess that it is because we will always show the cause of death as being what actually killed us (pneumonia, lung disease) when the true cause of the illness was due to the body's own immune system not being able to fight off what it normally would have, had it not been so weak. So we won't say he or she died of HIV because it's too embarrassing. We'll say that he or she died of the symptom that was blown up by the HIV.

We cannot be embarrassed. The truth brings attention to this crisis. This embarrassment can help a lot of people. Easier said than done. Even I would have a tough time of it. Africa is now talking about it. That's good, but that's only the beginning. A good beginning to reduce the spread of AIDS considerably. America, black America especially, has to face this. Our future is at stake. While we are fighting each other today, there is something in our culture today that is killing us tomorrow. My people perish not only from the lack of wisdom but from the fear of facing and discussing our problems. Problems in the black community that only the black community can solve. God is waiting for us to cry out honestly instead of acting out in shame. To ask the right questions, seek the right answers, knock down doors that separate us. God can heal us from the inside out. He is not asking for perfection or results right now, just effort. Just close your eyes and reach out. God is never further away than the length of your outstretched arms. Never!

The Faces of South Africa

Every face, every person, everybody has value. We are living, breathing human beings regardless of our color, status, age, look, wealth, ethnicity, or anything else. We must value one another's worth and make the connection to our future. While you may be upset or mad at any person for any reason, taking away their life is never your right. It is never the solution. You must realize that when a bullet enters a person, there is a very good chance that that person's life will either be changed forever or that person will die. That person is just like you. They have family and people that love them. Don't take a life for no good or lawful reason. Learn to stay in control.

Our hope is in knowing who our real enemy is and defeating it with love, lest we be consumed.

Dem Boots

While on the job, after sixteen years, one day there was a major change that came into effect almost overnight. There was a change in guard at the CEO level due to many unsatisfied customers throughout the years. This was a collection agency, and the prevailing attitude among the troops, in reference to those who didn't pay, was, "They owe us and won't pay, so why should we cut them any slack?" Now, this organization was black heavy, if you know what I mean. Blacks and minorities made up a significant number of the labor force. So when the word came down that all of the slack had been pulled in on the rope that connected us—and that means everyone—to this organization, well let's just say we were not pleased. No one was, but you can imagine who the monkeys were on the line and who would ultimately be first and unfairly affected by any shakedowns or changes.

The changes were put in place in order to accomplish one particular goal: to make the customer number one. To create a belief in and confidence of the customer that they would be treated fairly and consistently no matter what, regardless of their past sins. Now to pull this off, the troops would have to adopt an entirely new mind-set. The way of doing business had to change. And you know how people take to change. New objectives were written. New policies adopted. A new mission statement was put into place. People who could were taking early retirement, and some simply left midstream. Fear ran its course all through the organization. The biggest concern was that most of the new rules and regulations were geared toward consequences upon the employees for any indiscretions committed against any client, representative of the client, or anyone connected to the investigation or collection. Training was too quick and too brief, and the new rules seemed so impossible that the prevailing opinion among all (especially among blacks and "disposable" whites) was that we were all being set up to fail. There was simply no way to achieve the perfection and accuracy required of us, all knowing that the consequences of our sins would be immediate dismissal without due process. No questions asked. It was also our responsibility to read up on all of the rules because saying "I didn't know" was unacceptable.

So one day I took some time to seriously look over these rules, and indeed they required every I to be dotted and every T to be crossed. But ironically, I caught myself saying something that would turn my fears into strength. It changed my whole way of thinking about this situation. The statement I uttered under my breath was, "These people are trying to make us professionals or something!"

I then reflected back on a business meeting I attended at a church. More specifically, something I heard the pastor say in that predominantly black church. After going over the business plans, application of donations, and future plans laid out for the church and surrounding community, I realized that the pastor was very optimistic (otherwise known as faith) in the goals for the church. This was a multimillion-dollar venture. It would take an unflinching group of faithful, God-fearing individuals to pull it off. He informed us that he had put together a very special group of people he gave a specific title to. He said that he had informed them, all a part of the elder board, that he expected them to rise to a higher level of technical excellence. He explained that his greatest fear was that the anticipated ministry or project he was embarking on would outgrow the ability for it to be properly managed. Unless the level of its managers—elders, deacons, and lay ministers—consistently rose in technical excellence above the growth of the ministry, it would be uncontrollable and therefore not used to its full capacity, or worse, it would fail. He was trapped behind the eight ball he had created. The moral to this story? You must grow consistently larger and become technically excellent in efficiency *with* the big picture, or the big picture will swallow you up. That, I believe with all my heart, is the greatest problem in the demise and stunting of the American Negro.

As was in Egypt with the children of Israel, Negroes in America who unwillingly participated in the physical and mental slavery of years past knew who the enemy was. The enemy was whipping them across their backs, treating them like cattle, raping their wives, and abusing their children in front of them. After slavery, the enemies were the ones denying Negroes access, liberties of life, and an education. But now there is no admitted physical slavery in America, freedom has been restored, education allowed, and there is access to just about anything one can dream about. So why are we still not free? Why do we now enslave ourselves with denials, names, ridicules, and lack of respect? We are free, we are educated or have access to an education, and we are professionals with the ability to financially empower others and ourselves—lawyers to defend others and ourselves, teachers to educate others and ourselves. We have made great strides and have stood the tests of time to the surprise and astonishment of others, including the enemy. But now is the time to stop blaming the enemy. They are not the cause of who we are or are not today. We are. It's almost as if we have taken up where the enemy left off. We now call each other nigger, dog, and boy. We now avoid doing business with our people.

We now whip one another, talk to one another like cattle, and mistreat our wives and children. I believe it's because we fail to hold ourselves accountable. Accountable to what? To a higher level of consistent growth. To a higher level of technical excellence. We have allowed the big picture to swallow us up. We need a drastic change in the rules with little room to fail. We need to tighten up the reins on ourselves and our way of doing business. We must speak out about ourselves and our "slovern" way of dressing, respecting, and doing business. We must increase the level of expectation of ourselves as a people. We must stop accepting bad customer service, un-manicured businesses, unacceptable name-calling, and what I call Feminized Men and Masculine Women syndrome. We are equal as men and women in humanity, respect and before God, but we are different in hierarchy, expectation, duty and physical capabilities in many cases. We must accept that as black men and black women. We all must accept that as children of God.

Stop the silent, disrespectful competition. Stop the liberated separation between the sexes. We must unite in knowledge and finances. We must also begin to compliment one another's efforts, accept our results, and help one another to do better. We must start taking care of ourselves personally through exercise for our bodies as well as our minds. Too many of us are overweight and dying too soon because of what we eat. Without moderation the stereotypical soul foods connected to our race, such as barbecue, ham, beer, and other strong drinks, are killing us about as fast as we are killing ourselves. While it stirs our soul, it is destroying our bodies. There is an alarming increase of black men, especially, having heart attacks in their late thirties and early forties, mostly due to high blood pressure, high cholesterol, and an unknown history of stroke and heart attacks in their families. Not to mention the number of our black women suffering the same, as well as the agonies and pains of cancer, primarily breast cancer. How can we as a people, who have gone through so much, dare to expect others to respect us when we clearly show the world that we don't respect ourselves?

Dem boots were made for walkin', or dem boots are going to walk all over you.

"A Room with a View"

There once was a room with a view
That offered the whole world to you;
A window and chair
Just sitting there
To wake up the child in you.

Excited but very afraid,
You sat there for hours and days.
You'd been there for so long
Afraid to go on,
Trapped in this mindless gaze.

Your will to move forward was tested.
Only time did you have invested.
God spoke to you
In this room with a view
And told you that you were selected.

He remembered the promise He made.
You accepted Him; now you are saved.
Get up from that chair,
Wake up from that stare,
And go to the window He gave.

Life is beautiful thing,
But it's not for you to cling
To all that it gives
In order to live
This life of drugs and bling, bling.

There's a door in that room with a view
That is eager to offer you
More choices to make,
Some real and some fake,
But the choices are all up to you.

Remember, you're never alone,
So don't be afraid to go on.
Your past is behind you,
Your future's ahead.
Can't wait till you get to go home.

There once was a room with a view
That offered the whole world to you;
A window and chair
Just sitting there
To wake up the child in you.

God loves you, still.

The book of Matthew, chapter 22, verses 36–40, explains what I consider the foundation of human existence. In an attempt to trip Jesus up, one of the Pharisees asked Jesus this question: "Teacher, which is the great commandment in the Law?" Notice he said great, not greatest, commandment in the law (exclusivity). Put a pin in that for right now. Jesus answered, "You shall love the Lord your God with all your heart, and with all your soul, and with all your mind. This is the great and foremost commandment." Notice He said "and foremost" (i.e., greatest) commandment (inclusivity). And for free, Jesus offered this saying, "The second is like it, 'You shall love your neighbor as yourself.' On these two commandments depend the whole Law and Prophets."

What this says to me is that the entire foundation of the law rests on loving God and loving your neighbor. With the absence of one or both of these, the rest of the laws are without support because these two are the foundation that the other laws rest on, and without love, you have a cracked foundation. Always shaky, always moving. To love God first is to know what love is. To love your neighbor is our challenge, to demonstrate that love, or to know how to love, in preparation for heaven itself. You must recognize who your neighbor is. This has to start with ourselves. As black people, we act as though we hate who we are, as if we hate ourselves. We are first our own neighbors. Love does indeed include the greater population, but love must first start at home. We have left our first love. God. As a result, we have forgotten how and whom to love. We have forgotten what love is. Even more importantly, we have forgotten the destruction the absence of love causes. Or maybe that is the only thing we do remember, which is why we are so angry.

We can't reinvent love. If we don't love ourselves—and we prove that by being so destructive to ourselves—and if we feel that we have neighbors that don't love us, we will continue to consume one another until there is nothing left, passing this on to future generations. I believe Jesus died for those first two commandments, knowing that without the spread of love for God and for our neighbors, all else is sinking sand. For us to not love ourselves and for others to not love us—as well as our loving them—is breaking the two greatest commandments we have. It also breaks the heart of God.

There is a song sung by Hezekiah Walker with these haunting words:

I love you.
I'll pray for you.
You are important to me.
I need you to survive.

Can you look at your brother or sister and say that? Believe that? Need that?

Love—need—survive.
You better get this into your system!
Or be consumed.

Consumed by One Another

Let's break the silence about ourselves. Whether black or white, fire consumes all in its path. Racism kills. Hatred hinders progress. Let's just be honest with ourselves—for a *change*.

Acknowledgments

My mother, Sylvia M. Walker, who showed me that fear and people can get in the way of where you really want to go and what you really want to do, and, though life doesn't seem fair always, with God anything is possible, as long as He has the last word.

My beautiful and wonderful daughter, Ashley, of whom I am most proud and who is my silent inspiration, motivation, and greatest investment. Life would not be the same without you. Cling to God. He will protect you in ways that I can't.

Writers and thinkers and doers who stare fear and hesitation in the face and say and do and write what is morally right, mentally challenging, and forward thinking. You give me courage. You are too many to count.

To the most important voice of all, the voice of my Lord and Savior Jesus Christ, who gives me hope, patience, love, peace, grace, and mercy. Speak to me, oh Lord. Speak to me. I do not deserve Your love.

Current and Upcoming Works by DSWalker

Just Us, Notes from a black child's father
My story about tragedy, blessings, and the needs and struggles of black single fathers. (Currently out of circulation, soon to be republished.)

What'cha Lookin' For?
A book that explores some answers to our dreams, hopes, and future goals and why we oftentimes fall short. (Not yet published.)

White Flight, Black Butterfly
A journey based on a true story about a young, gifted, and beautiful black girl who, while being let down by the men in her life put there to protect her, grew up in a world that caused her to question her blackness and worth at the expense of her soul. Available now in your ebook.com stores.

Why Can't You Mind Your Own Business!
Practical reasons and answers to owning a business in a world where failure looks to be a common thing. It doesn't have to be. (Soon to be published.)

Beware of the Locust
A book about putting your life in perspective. (Not yet published.)

Hearing Voices: Man's search for common sense (Not yet published.)

A Story a Day Keeps the Devil Away, a children's book. (Not yet published.)

Consumed by One Another

To order copies of this book: eBook it through search engines or request it through your local bookstore(s). Available at amazon.com and barnesandnoble.com as well.

Printed in the United States
By Bookmasters